The Number 1 Inspirational Chiropractic Books Best Seller
INTRODUCTION BY JAMES BLAIR HILL, DO

INSPIRE
CHIROPRACTIC

Based on the Original 1937 Version of
Napoleon Hill's Best Selling Classic
Think And Grow Rich

Includes Special Interview with
Mark Victor Hansen
Co-Creator of The Chicken Soup Series

Dr. Matt Hammett
&
Dr. Trish Hammett

"This small volume is a testament to the success philosophy of Napoleon Hill. It is filled with riches of life, and its philosophy permeates the very substance of what we call chiropractic."

-Dr. Matt Hammett

www.InspireChiropractic.net

Inspire Chiropractic

Based on the 1937 original edition of *Think and Grow Rich*

*   *   *   *

"Although, Napoleon Hill was born more than a century ago, and wrote his most influential book more than seventy years ago, *Chiropractic Riches* shows that his work has as much relevance today as it did when he partnered with Dr. William Harris."
Dr. James Blair Hill
(*Napoleon Hill's grandson*)

*   *

BY

DR. MATT HAMMETT
&
DR. TRISH HAMMETT

*

2010
Originally Published by Dr. Matt Hammett

All Rights Reserved

Printed in the U.S.A.

With Introduction
By James Blair Hill DO

Cover Design by
Dr. Matt Hammett

Published by
Dr. Matt Hammett
P.O. Box 11988
Merrillville, IN 46410

Copyright© 2010-2011 by Dr. Matt Hammett

All Rights Reserved

Scripture quotations are from:
The Douay-Rheims Bible.

Napoleon Hill photograph:
New York World-Telegram and the Sun Newspaper Photograph Collection (Library of Congress)

ISBN: 978-0-615-34194-1

This book is based on the facsimile of the complete and original edition of Think and Grow Rich by Napoleon Hill, originally published by The Ralston Society in 1937 and now in the public domain.

This book and its teaching make many references to the classic 1937 book "Think And Grow Rich" by Napoleon Hill. THINK AND GROW RICH® is the registered trademark and property of the Napoleon Hill Foundation. The book title "Think And Grow Rich" and any references are being used for illustrative purposes only, without permission and are not authorized by, associated with, endorsed by, or sponsored by the Napoleon Hill Foundation. Any reference to "Think And Grow Rich" is by necessity in referring to the book title.

All rights reserved. No part of this book may be reproduced by any mechanical, photographic, or electronic process or in the form of a phonographic recording; nor may it be stored in a retrieval system, transmitted, or otherwise be copied for public or private use without prior written permission of the publisher.

The authors of this book does not dispense medical advice or prescribe the use of any technique as a form of treatment for physical, emotional, or medical problems without the advice of a physician, either directly or indirectly. The intent of the authors is only to offer information of a general nature to help you in your journey of life. In the event you use any of the information in this book for yourself, which is your constitutional right, the authors and the publisher assume no responsibility for your actions.

This books title was originally called *Chiropractic Riches*. It has been changed to *Inspire Chiropractic* in order to reflect the opinions from various readers and reviewers.

Printed in the United States of America

This book is dedicated to...

William Harris DC
1918-2008
(Napoleon Hill's late chiropractor)

&

Napoleon Hill
1883-1970
(Author of Best Selling Book: *Think and Grow Rich*)

Memorandum

"Dr. Harris, Mr. Hill, Dr. Lorraine Golden, Mr. Stone and Dr. Lipke"

*

"Mr. W. Clement Stone, Chicago Insurance executive with Dr. William Harris Director of Public Relations for Kentuckiana."

'Do-It' Day at Toledo brought an enthusiastic reception from the over 250 doctors, wives and receptionists who attended.

The laymen's meeting held at a local high school on the evening prior to the Sunday 'Do-It' Day saw 700 people in the audience.

Mr. Napoleon Hill, author of Think and Grow Rich, intrigued his listeners with his personal experiences and philosophy which led to the writing of this book. This volume has sold over ten million copies and Mr. Hill's newest book, Success Through A Positive Mental Attitude is already well on the way to another record sales figure.

Dr. Bill Harris of Albany, Georgia, publicity director of Kentuckiana Children's Chiropractic Center, the organization which receives all proceeds from these meetings was lavish in his praise of the Ohio chiropractors who headed the 'Do-It' Day movement in their area.

Outstanding on the program of speakers was Dr. Ed. Reinhart of Kitchener, Ontario, Canada. Dr. Loraine Golden and the Ladies in Blue brought as their guest one of the children patients from the Center in Louisville.

Radio, television and newspaper publicity was excellent and very favorable on behalf of the chiropractic profession as the sponsors of this public service movement.

Local arrangements were under the direction of Dr. and Mrs. Thompson of Toledo. State publicity was headed by Dr. John Blossom of Montpelier, Ohio.

(Adapted from www.nicr.org Kentuckiana CHRONO 04/05/11)

Table of contents

Introduction		1
Chapter 1	(Mark Victor Hansen)	5
Chapter 2	(William Esteb)	22
Chapter 3	(Dr. Bob Hoffman)	34
Chapter 4	(Dr. Fabrizio Mancini)	46
Chapter 5	(Dr. Janice Hughes)	57
Chapter 6	(Dr. Dennis Perman)	67
Chapter 7	(Dr. Joan Fallon)	82
Chapter 8	(Dr. Larry Markson)	92
Chapter 9	(Dr. John F. Demartini)	106
Chapter 10	(Dr. Patrick Gentempo, Jr.)	123
Chapter 11	(Dr. Tedd Koren)	134
Epilogue	(Dr. Bobby Doscher)	146

An Introduction

By Dr. James B. Hill

(Napoleon Hill's Grandson)

"The authors show that the principles for success have not changed and neither has the need for personal achievement to sustain the business side of chiropractic."
- **Dr. James Blair Hill**

Dr. Hill, born in Morgantown, W.Va., is the son of David Hill, the youngest son of Napoleon Hill and Florence Hornor. He graduated from high school in 1966 and spent time in the Merchant Marines until 1969, when he was drafted into service as a private with the United States Marine Corps.

By 1973, he had been promoted five times to the rank of staff sergeant and given the opportunity to attend Vanderbilt University, where he earned a bachelor's degree in mechanical engineering. At graduation, he was commissioned as a second lieutenant and commenced service in the Marines as a field artillery officer. He later earned a master's degree in mathematics from the Naval Postgraduate School.

As an officer, he held command twice, led a team of military advisors into Southeast Asia, briefed the Soviet General Staff, served as aide-de-camp to two Marine Corps generals, taught mathematics at the U.S. Naval Academy, and served in many critical billets at the battery, battalion, and regimental level. He is certified in scuba, mountain, cold weather, and jungle warfare and is a graduate of the Army's Command and General Staff College.

In 1995, he retired from the Marine Corps after 26 years of service to study medicine. At the age of 53, he graduated from medical school and started a three-year residency in family medicine. Dr. Hill is now board-certified in family medicine and holds certifications in wound care and hyperbaric medicine.

He lives with his wife and two children in Bridgeport, WV.

Special Introduction:

The relationship between Napoleon Hill and Chiropractic is part of the history of the profession. However, it is also much more than history; it remains to this day a sustaining force that continues to propagate wherever chiropractic is practiced. Not long ago, I introduced myself to a local chiropractor who was displaying one of Napoleon Hill's quotations on an office sign. He told me that his practice succeeded because he followed the principles that Napoleon Hill discussed in *Think and Grow Rich*. He told me that it was not enough for a chiropractor to be skillful at healing. A chiropractor must be that, of course, but he also needs to be a businessman and for that he needs the skills of personal achievement given to us by Napoleon Hill.

This young chiropractor along with the authors are part of a new generation of chiropractors who understand that chiropractic has a business side that is just as important to the profession as the ability to deliver quality care. William Harris, DC recognized this during the early 1950's when he discovered that an alarming number of chiropractors closed their practice because of business failure. He established a foundation to promote chiropractic and to provide consulting services for ailing practices.

In 1960, William Harris was the director of public relations for the Kentuckiana Children's Chiropractic Center and sponsoring seminars to provide inspiration and practical advice to both doctors and laymen to advance the profession. He brought in Napoleon Hill as a guest speaker and thus began the very close relationship between Napoleon Hill and chiropractic. For the next two years, Napoleon Hill attended William Harris seminars and workshops across the country to teach the principles of success that have proven so essential for chiropractic. It was during this time that Napoleon Hill became forever associated with chiropractic.

While I credit William Harris, DC for this relationship, chiropractic was hardly new to Napoleon Hill. In the 1920's Napoleon Hill advertised chiropractic in his "Napoleon Hill's Magazine." He also advertised the Palmer School of Chiropractic to prospective students. He seems to have had a very close relationship with B. J. Palmer, DC who became a mentor that embodied many of the Hill's principles of personal achievement. Palmer was his personal chiropractor until 1961 when he passed away. This personal relationship makes it likely that Hill took his son Blair to Palmer for the chiropractic care that played such a pronounced role in Blair's success at overcoming his disability. After Palmer died in 1961, Hill turned to William Harris for chiropractic care.

So the relationship between Napoleon Hill and chiropractic was both personal and professional. His work with William Harris, DC forged a weld so strong that generations of chiropractors have now been exposed to the tools needed to succeed in advancing chiropractic. *Inspire Chiropractic* provides fascinating insight to the legacy of the Hill/Harris partnership.

Borrowing a page from Napoleon Hill, the authors interviewed some of the most influential men and women involved in chiropractic over the past 20 years. However, unlike Napoleon Hill, the authors present their findings as a collation of interviews that does not distill information. This leaves the personality of each interviewee intact to savor. The result is a fascinating aggregate of stories collected from vibrant men and women who have lived and are still living successful lives.

These stories show a profound relationship between the success each achieved and Napoleon Hill's science of personal achievement. Although at least one of these people achieved success without prior exposure to *Think and Grow Rich*, all of them employed his principles.

I recently discovered the baccalaureate address that Napoleon Hill gave at Salem College in 1957. The speech is titled the "The Five Essentials of Success" and lists as essentials:

Definite of purpose

The Mastermind

Going the extra mile

Self-discipline

Applied faith

Napoleon Hill's steps for success later evolved into his seventeen principles for success. It follows then that these "essentials" are clearly the five most important of Napoleon Hill's seventeen principles of success.

The authors of *Inspire Chiropractic* ask each interviewee which step is the most important and why. As you read the answers, you will find an incredible correlation between what these men and women believe is important to success and Napoleon Hill's five essentials for success. The strength of this correlation is no doubt the reason why Napoleon Hill's "steps" for success later evolved into "principles" for success.

Although, Napoleon Hill was born more than a century ago, and wrote his most influential book more than seventy years ago, *Inspire Chiropractic* shows that his work has as much relevance today as it did when he partnered with William Harris. The authors show that the principles for success have not changed and neither has the need for personal achievement to sustain the business side of chiropractic.

Inspire Chiropractic is a delightful storybook. Enjoy.

Chapter 1

MARK VICTOR HANSEN
Co-creator of Chicken Soup for the Soul Series

"You can easily create the life you deserve."
— Mark Victor Hansen

*F*ocused solely on helping people from all walks of life reshape their vision of what's possible, no one is better respected in the area of human potential than Mark Victor Hansen. Creating powerful change in thousands of organizations and millions of individuals worldwide for over 30 years, Mark delivers proven messages of possibility, opportunity and action.

You may know Mark as "that Chicken Soup for the Soul guy." Established as a cultural icon in 1990, Mark and his business partner Jack Canfield created what *Time* magazine called, "**the publishing phenomenon of the decade**," with over 110 million *Chicken Soup for the Soul* books sold worldwide – one of the most successful publishing franchises of all time.

Internationally known keynote speaker and personality. With his one-of-a-kind technique and masterful authority of his work, time and again he receives high accolades from his audiences as one of the most dynamic and compelling speakers of our time. Having spoken in more than 60 countries, Mark has shared his message of opportunity and action and created powerful transformation in thousands of organizations and millions of individuals worldwide.

Inspire Chiropractic

While the Chicken Soup series has achieved phenomenal success, Mark's other bestselling books include *The One Minute Millionaire, Cracking the Millionaire Code, How to Make the Rest of Your Life the Best of Your Life, The Aladdin Factor, Dare to Win* and *The Power of Focus*. Mark has also developed an extensive library of audio and video programs in the areas of big thinking, sales achievement, publishing success and personal and professional development.

His endearing and charismatic style captures audiences' hearts as well as their attention in person, on television or radio and in print.

> Appearances – Oprah, CNN, The Today Show, and countless television, print and radio interviews
> Quoted in- *Time, U.S. News & World Report, USA Today, New York Times, and Entrepreneur*

Expanding his business ventures and leading by example, Mark launched Hansen House publishing in 2008, bringing the most compelling ideas from the world's greatest thinkers to print.
Further, he has targeted the realms of television and feature film for his next steps in his own journey.

Through his library of audios, videos, and articles in the areas of big thinking, sales achievement, wealth building, publishing success and personal and professional development, Mark continues to create a profound influence.

Coaching and teaching aspiring authors, speakers and experts on building lucrative publishing and speaking careers through his MEGA seminar series, Mark produces top-notch, results oriented annual conferences.
Recipient of numerous awards honoring his entrepreneurial spirit, philanthropic heart and business acumen Mark was inducted into the Sales & Marketing Executive International Hall of Fame and accepted the Horatio Alger Award for extraordinary life achievement in the area of free enterprise leadership.

Working tirelessly for organizations such as Habitat for Humanity, American Red Cross, March of Dimes and Childhelp USA and establishing his own foundation dedicated to literacy as a means to end poverty, Mark firmly believes that giving back is paramount to his own personal happiness and success. He is

Mark Victor Hansen

proud to be the recipient of the Visional Philanthropist for Youth Award by Covenant House of California (2004) among others.

Notes from the editors:

Last year, my family was getting ready to go on a well-deserved vacation to Cancun, when my mother-in-law fell ill with a mysterious ailment and paralysis took over her body. The illness, eventually diagnosed as Guillain-Barre Syndrome, swept into the hearts of us all for days. Today, she has fully recovered but only after six months of intense physical therapy. I remember it well. I had just buried my father after a long battle of prostate cancer. He shared with me one of my forgotten dreams: to be an author; and before he passed away, he told me how proud he was of my being a chiropractor. He also shed some light on the death of my older brother, who died when he was six years of age after taking an aspirin. With his last spoken words to me, my dad revealed his pride and his vision of seeing me influence the world as a chiropractor, a parent, a husband, and as an author.

I was overwhelmed; and, during the last seconds of my father's passing, somehow I knew it was his time. I gripped my father's hand and wiped the last tear from his eyes. Then, I promised him that I would never again settle for mediocrity, that I would strive to be better in this world, *for* this world, and that I would somehow fulfill my childhood dream of becoming an author.

> "My own experience with failure happened when I went bankrupt and lost $2 million in one day in 1974. I felt like a miserable failure and hid under the covers for six months. Then I started listening to tapes and reading books like *Think & Grow Rich* and started attending seminars and ultimately giving seminars, and now I think I've talked to five million people live at over 4,000 talks around the world."
>
> -Mark Victor Hansen

Inspire Chiropractic

A few weeks later, my wife returned from a Mark Victor Hansen seminar with an audio package titled *Mega Book Marketing*. I was excited; but, how would I find time to listen to and study this program with a newborn child to care for, and what about my current work schedule? The answer followed shortly, we already had a week's vacation scheduled after my mother-in-law fell ill, so my wife attended to her mother, while I took care of our son and worked on the book seminar.

When my son took his naps, I could study. I poured through the seminar; and, toward the end of it, I had a vision. That vision was this book, and I could see in my mind which people I would invite to interview for this book. Somehow, we managed to involve everyone on the original list I had created. Beginning two years prior to the actual writing, I have studied, edited and tested the principles laid out in this book.

At the time I began writing, I was an associate, working for someone else. I was doing well, but I lacked the personal time I desired. However, since the application of the philosophy discussed here and the use of these time-tested principles you are about to read, I have joined my wife on an entrepreneurial adventure. Today, after applying the principles contained in this book, we have experienced improvements to our finances, relationships, and to our social, physical, and spiritual well-being. The more I have read this little book and listened to the audio interviews, the more these principles have taken over my life. Now, I am proud to share with you some of the discoveries that I have made, I and look forward to seeing you at the top!

-Dr. Matt Hammett

Dr. Trish Hammett interviewing Mark Victor Hansen:

We are here with Mark Victor Hansen, co-creator of *Chicken Soup for the Soul series*. He is also a prolific author of many books, including *The One-Minute Millionaire* and *Cracking the Millionaire Code*. He is also a very well known national and international speaker and the creator of the Mega Seminars. Welcome.

Thank you for having me.

Can you tell us how you were introduced to Napoleon Hill's *Think & Grow Rich*?

Mark Victor Hansen

The first time I heard of it, I was listening to a mandatory convocation in college. We had an ex-convict named Bill Sands speak to us. He had done all sorts of terrible things to get the attention of his parents. His nose was pressed to his face because when he went to the federal penitentiary, they tried to do things he couldn't accept, so they broke his nose and his fingers. Then Warden Clinton Duffy came up to him and said, "Boy, you are way too smart to be here. We just tested you, and you are off the Richter scale. If you'll read this little book called *Think & Grow Rich*, it'll change your life."

I went out and bought the book, read it, and misunderstood it because I was a little too superficial. I imagined that if I had a goal of making $50,000 a year, I could write that on a board and hang it next to the wall in my little trailer at the university. That would be the key to achieving success. However, it didn't work. I kept the book anyway and I kept reading it, the concepts finally clicked.

I truly understood Napoleon Hill when I went bankrupt in 1974. I was building geodesic domes in New York, and when I was completely wrecked, I took the book and studied it intensively with a guy named Chip Collins. On page 36, the book exhorted its readers to do six things, which I implemented in my life immediately. Then Bob Proctor and I put into practice every word in the book. It was a good philosophy.

Can you tell us how this book and its philosophies influenced your life?

Napoleon Hill called himself the millionaire maker and made more people rich than anyone else. He studied the 500 greats, like Andrew Carnegie.

I've read all of Carnegie's classic stuff, and I've been to Andrew Carnegie's house in New York at 91st and Fifth Avenue. I spent $4,000 a day to go to Andrew Carnegie's house in Dornoch, Scotland, which is 30,000 acres. Andy was the richest man in the world because he owned Bethlehem Steel. Napoleon Hill was a 17-year-old kid when he interviewed him. At the end of the interview, Andy said, "I want somebody to do the philosophy of personal achievement and success. I'll introduce you to the 500 most important people in the world. By the way, I'm not going to pay you anything for it." Napoleon said, "Yes, I will do it," Andy

Inspire Chiropractic

pulled out his watch and Napoleon took exactly 29 seconds to decide. He said, "If it took you over 30 seconds to make the decision, you'd be a failure. You must be instantaneously decisive. You've got to decide in favor of yourself, go for the gusto, decide you're going to do the juice, and then live up to what your commitments are."

So he spent the next three days at his house interviewing him, then gave him the names of the other people he needed to interview. The information later became the book *How to Raise Your Own Salary*. If you haven't read it, you've got to read it. It's a profound book.

Tell us about your background with chiropractic and your relationship with the chiropractic profession.

"You've got to be rich in who you are as a being. You've got to be a big being. Most people are being small or far less than who they could be."

The first time I saw a chiropractor, I was 28 years old and living in Boulder, Colorado. I had never heard of chiropractic, but I started befriending chiropractors and eventually started going to a chiropractor named Steve Dunbar D.C. He suggested that I talk to chiropractors. I did some local talks in Orange County and found that we were philosophically the same, top-down, inside-out.

Then I had a chiropractor named Dr. Gary Cochere D.C. come over to our house and have dinner on a regular basis. One time I sprained my ankle as I was running and Gary noticed my crutches during dinner. Gary asked, "Any torn ligaments show up in the x-rays?" When I told him there weren't, he said, "Then get off the crutches and sit down." He did extremities adjustment. I thought, "I've got to tell people in the world this, because nobody knows this exists." That was when I decided to be an external advocate for chiropractic.

"The book exhorted its readers to do six things, which I

10

Mark Victor Hansen

I started giving talks. I was going quarterly over to talk at Life Chiropractic and Dynamic Essentials meetings, and went regularly for Dr. Jim Parker at Parker Seminars. Then I started talking at all the universities, and amazingly, the students were enthusiastic. They were buying all our *Chicken Soup* books and loved them (after all, everybody wants to overcome their diversities). It was an amazing experience. I eventually got three honorary doctorates in chiropractic.

Once you have got a book done, generally, publishers are slow to accept it. Usually they take a year-and-a-half to get a book out, which is just like the movie business. We did not have any money since we both put $140,000 into the *Chicken Soup* series. Then my ex-wife told me, "You like all the chiropractors and you know what they do, and thanks to Bill Clinton there's no insurance, so why don't you plan how to run a cash practice?"

I soon interviewed with a few top doctors, two of whom were running million dollar practices and just doing an absolutely brilliant job. I went out and sold so many that I couldn't believe it. One of the guys I interviewed was Dr. Dennis Nikitow in Denver. He always had rubber bands in his pocket. He would say to people, "Here's a rubber band. Wrap it around your index finger and if you tie it, we are going to call this subluxation. If you don't take it off, what happens?" They would always say, "Your finger goes blue, purple, and then black, and then it falls off." He would answer: "That's correct. So who can get rid of that? Can a doctor get rid of it? No. Can a PT, a physical therapist, get rid of it? No. Can a massage therapist? No. Who's the only doctor who can get rid of it? A chiropractor." It was such an easy sale and such a wondrous thing to teach.

I was spreading the chiropractic message, and then I started doing a wonderful thing called chiropractic appreciation day. Sort of like what Napoleon Hill did during the height of the depression: he would start talking in a restaurant that didn't have anyone eating in it and just created business like crazy. It was amazing. Once in Chicago he was on a program with W. Clement Stone who was running a company that was bringing in $3 million a year. Stone, who had read *Think & Grow Rich* said, "Oh my God, you're good. Why don't you come in and train all my people?" In one year, this company went from $3 million to $170 million.

This stuff works. What happens is most people don't have clear wants and desires. It is not enough to want something. You

Inspire Chiropractic

should strive for it and will it. You say, "I don't want to be poor," but if you keeping thinking, "I'm poor, I'm poor, I can't afford to pay my bills," then sure enough, you'll go bankrupt and lose it all.

In *Think & Grow Rich*, the publisher's preface states that riches cannot always be measured in terms of money. We'd like to hear your thoughts on that statement and what your personal definition of being rich is.

You can be rich in health, which is the most important thing, from a chiropractic point of view. We call it "well being." Well being is always flowing, so you have to be in tune with the infinite, in tune with well being, and in tune with the innate, as we call it in chiropractic. I'm rich in health. I'm 61 years young and I just did yoga for an hour-and-a-half and then I went to the chiropractor afterwards because I got a little disc out, so I've got to go back again one more time today. The fact that I'm doing this meeting with you today is amazing.

I think you ought to be rich in telling yourself that you're going to feel good, because feeling good is everything and feeling joy is the most profound job in life. Next, I think you've got to decide that you're going to make a phenomenal contribution.

So there are four basic aspects of being rich: You've got to be rich in who you are as a being. You've got to be a big being. Most people are being small or far less than who they could be. Then you've got to be passionate and purposeful. You've got to be big in your relationship, and you've got to do something that's bigger than you are. In other words, if all I want to do is go to work for a measly, little amount of money, come home and watch TV, crush beer cans on my head and throw them in the back of the SUV, that wouldn't be a fulfilling life. When Jack and I did *Chicken Soup for the Grieving Soul*, which I think sold at every mortuary, cemetery, and crematory in America; we interviewed all the top doctors of death and dying: Elizabeth Kubler-Ross, Steven Levine, and so on. They said each of them had held 20,000 people that went to the other side, went to the light, and came back. The people with any regrets were the ones who didn't do good things, not those who did bad things.

Do you feel that being rich and being successful is the same thing?

Mark Victor Hansen

Nope. I define success differently than anybody else on the planet. Success is the difference between the utilization of your full potential and how much you're utilizing now. You've got potential spiritually, mentally, physically, financially, emotionally, and socially. To become a fully-functioning human being, you've got to work on all those areas a little bit on a daily basis. When one of them gets too out of kilter, which happens to everyone, you've got to go back and work on it more.

Do you happen to have a personal motto for success?

I don't really affirm that I'm successful. I suppose I did in the old days. When I was absolutely dead-ass broke, I used to convince myself that I was rich, healthy, wealthy, happy, that I felt terrific, that I was doing exactly what I wanted to do and it was being done with effortless ease and joy. I was living with passion and hanging out with people that made a lasting, impactful, permanent, and important difference.

> "According to the Guinness Book of Records, I'm the world's best selling non-fiction author."

That's where I am today. Obviously, having sold 157,000,000 books (and according to the Guinness Book of Records, I'm the world's best selling non-fiction author), I've done well. But that's just a beginning.

That's why success is elusive. So many idiots out there think they should retire. That's why I wrote a book with Art Linkletter – he's a 96-year-old human icon that is running the world's biggest solar energy company with 28 patents on the sun and 20,000 employees. At 96, he is healthier than most 40-year-olds. What we say about retirement is if you retire, you expire. We don't want you to retire. We want you to re-fire, either at the job you did and did well because we need you, or to take up a new occupation. That's what we really need; people to create intellectual property, the likes of which we've never had before. Everybody can do it. Everybody is a born entrepreneur. Or get into volunteering. The world has never needed more volunteerism than it needs now.

I think the psychic whammy that we're having financially is going to put a lot of people back. I've heard of three people over 70 who have lost all their wealth and have to go back to work.

Inspire Chiropractic

They're all bitching and moaning about it, which is the stupidest thing they could do. They ought to be happy that they've got a shot at going to work. They ought to be happy that they had a chance at retirement. They ought to be unhappy, maybe, that they lost their wealth in the stock market by being leveraged too much in Leman Brothers or Merrill Lynch, or something of the sort, but that's why you need to diversify your money. I've written in my books *One Minute Millionaire, Crack the Millionaire Code*, and in the two new ones, we've got coming out, *The Richest Kids in America* and *Fast Money in Slow Times*, that you've got to, have multiple streams of money and multiple projects. Everything in the universe has peaks and valleys. It has ups and downs. In quantum physics, things pulsate. If you don't expect night to follow day, you haven't been awake very long.

> "All your problems are profits in disguise."

If I was too caustic on those people who have lost their jobs, as a consolation, I am doing a new product today on how everyone can get their perfect, idyllic job. I've got this deep in my mind because of what Bernard said: "Find a need and fill it." I think Bernie had it wrong. I thing you should find a want and fill it, because people buy wants before they buy needs. You might need braces, if you're an alcoholic and you want a drink, you'll buy the drink first.

I just was at *Childhelp*. I raised a lot of money for them. It's one of the many charities I believe in, run by two brilliant mastermind women over in Arizona. Unfortunately, parents who take methamphetamines would rather stay on the drugs than feed their kids. That's why they immediately take children away from parents that are on meth. It's just atrocious. We've got to get people to stop using that crap.

In *Think & Grow Rich*, Napoleon Hill includes the following quote, "A peculiar thing about this secret of riches is that those who acquire it and use it find themselves literally swept on to success, but with little effort, and they never again submit to failure." We'd like to hear your thoughts on that.

It's really simple. The secret he's talking about is awareness – he called it thinking. What you've got to do is elevate your awareness. The point is that once you escalate up the hierarchy, a lot of things happen. First of all, you start having money and

Mark Victor Hansen

you look at the world differently. You've got to have money and the freedom to buy time, the freedom to get relationships, and the freedom to be spiritual so you know who you are in God and that God is in you. Finally, you can achieve creative freedom, which is the highest stance. In the beginning, God created the world, and you and I were made in the image and likeness of God. Then he said to us, "be fruitful, multiply," which is what we've done to the earth, which has now led to global warming. Now it's our job to use our intelligence, our awareness, our *Think & Grow Rich* to replenish the earth, which is what I'm about. I'm deeply invested in two alternative energy companies that are just booming.

> "Confront your fears and make them disappear. You've got to have goals that are so big, they thrill you and scare you to death."

My little example means that once you get rocking, you're going to get invited. You're going to start connecting. You're going to start having more stuff to do because as the scriptures say, "To whom much is given, much is required." You've always got to be the person you want to be. This is why Dr. Hill was always saying, "Go inside your mind before you go to sleep. Visualize the life you want and the lifestyle." I think it's the fourth principle. You could literally reach out and touch what we call in my newest book "virtualization," where you touch your dreams with your five inner senses: your inner sense of sight, your inner sense of hearing, your inner sense of smell, taste, and touch. You and I have to live with the assumption that our wishes will be fulfilled. That's how we change what we get out of it.

Pulling the concept of failure out of that quote, do you believe there's any such thing as failures in life, or are they just lessons to be learned?

Dr. Hill's exact line was, "every adversity has a seed of equivalent or greater benefit." I've rewritten it today to say "All your problems are profits in disguise." Hill meant that from a short view, things look like they're screwed up and not working. From a longer view, you might realize that things couldn't have worked out better than they did. My own experience with failure happened when I went bankrupt and lost $2 million in one day in 1974. I felt like a miserable failure and hid under the covers for six months. Then I started listening to tapes and reading books

Inspire Chiropractic

like *Think & Grow Rich* and started attending seminars and ultimately giving seminars, and now I think I've talked to five million people live at over 4,000 talks around the world. I'm heaviest now in China and in Russia. I see that Napoleon Hill was having the same kind of experience that I'm having. He was having the time of his life. He was getting to hang out with the 500 most important people, like Mr. Edison and Mr. Ford. He had uncommon friends, and when you have uncommon friends who do uncommon things, anything can happen.

Back to your earlier question. I'm hanging out with people that every once in a while make me step back and say, "Wow, that's cool." For instance, last year I was invited by Peter Guber to spend nine days after Christmas in his estate in Kauai. This guy has produced 228 Academy Award movies, including *Midnight Express, the Rocky movies, Batman, Flashdance*, and on and on. The who's who of the world was there, and I lodged for free for nine days on a 200-acre estate that he owns. It was better than any hotel I've ever been in. The food was marvelous. The company was like the head of *New Line Cinema*. I met Pierce Brosnan, the actor that plays *James Bond*. We just had a great time.

My parents were illiterate Danish people. My dad owned a little bakery that never made very much money because you don't make money selling five-cent rolls. Not that it was bad. We always ate and he loved my brothers and me. But I got a clean white T-shirt on Monday and another one on Thursday, and that was it. That's why at nine years old, I started selling and dreaming that someday, I'd be rich. So I had to attract *Think & Grow Rich* and this kind of thinking into my life so that I could not only score for me, but for others as well. Only the rich can help the poor. We desperately need to safely create as many wealthy people as possible, which is why my *One Minute Millionaire* is dedicated to creating a million millionaires by 2014 that will all give $1 million back to their church, charity, or its equivalent.

Now, of the thirteen steps that Napoleon Hill lists, he talks about desire, faith, auto-suggestion, specialized knowledge, imagination, organized planning, decision, persistence, power of the mastermind, the mystery of sex trans-mutation, the subconscious mind, the brain, and the sixth sense. Of these steps, which are a few of your favorite principles and why?

Mark Victor Hansen

The most critical one is your desire. It determines how high you're going to go. "What you think about comes about." In the beginning, I knew I wanted to be a speaker, so I thought about speaking, talked about speaking, and acted on speaking. If you got anywhere near me, that's all you heard about, and the questions I asked were about speaking. Then once I got the speaking thing sorted out and I found out where the market was, I became one of the founding members of the National Speakers Association. I would pick up every speaker in New York and drive him or her to their talk. I'd ask them endless questions. I had them all written out. I tape recorded it. I wanted it.

Then once I got going, I learned that you had to have a book to be really successful. When Robert suggested that we do a multi-author book together, I said I could do that. The guy sitting next to me was Keith DeGreen, now a very famous man who writes for many magazines. Keith and I ended up writing the first multi-authored book together. Jack and I have 212 multi-authored books called *Chicken Soup for the Soul*, for which I think we've had 58 number one slots in the *New York Times*. A lot of them should have been number one. We were number one in Singapore for the last 58 weeks with *Chicken Soup for the Singaporean Soul*.

Once you get going, a lot of cool things can happen, but you've got to get in motion and stay in motion.

He says that before you can put any of these steps into practice, you have to clear three enemies out of your mind. He lists those as indecision, doubt, and fear. Can you share with us some solutions you've used to clear those enemies out of your way?

Andrew Carnegie said if you can't make a decision in 30 seconds and stick to it, you're out, so you've got to be decisive.

The second one is doubt. "One percent doubt- you're out." You've got to be one hundred percent committed. I'm one hundred percent committed to my ideas and convictions.

Let me give you an example. Obviously, I've made a vast amount of money. I've been very charitable because we tithe in every one of our *Chicken Soup* books. I've even written a book called *The Miracle of Tithing*. I teach four Ts: tithe in your thinking, your time, your talent, and then your treasure is your

17

Inspire Chiropractic

money. I've raised all the blood I could for the American Red Cross a couple of times when they were out of blood. I sent an e-mail to all the chiropractors that said, "On this day, we're out of blood. We need 38,000 pints a day. We're only getting 19,000. I want you to adjust patients for free for giving blood. It's a community good will thing." I think we had 28,000 chiropractors call 1-800-Give-Life. We ought to do it again. Bring in a little blood mobile and collect blood. After all, if you get in a car accident or something and there's no blood at the hospital, you're simply dead. I keep giving blood and I'm good at it. You've got to be decisive. You can't have doubt. I never had any doubt that the chiropractors would do it, because you guys are the most generous people in the world.

The third one you have to do is confront your fears and make them disappear. You've got to have goals that are so big, they thrill you and scare you to death.

Everybody gives to charity when it's too damn late. You've got to do it at the front end, not at the back end when it's too late to make a difference. If we took care of people at the front end, they wouldn't have the back end problems.

I am doing two things: one is to end illiteracy, because literacy ends poverty. The only place poverty belongs is in a museum. Literacy is a critical issue. I watched my dad trying to read a men's room sign and having for a man to go in to know which bathroom was which. Nowadays we have symbols, but back when I was a little kid, they didn't have those. I decided to teach literacy over the telephone, and we're able to teach it fast. We're able to give a GED on the telephone with pictures, and that's going to help many Americans. Some little girl working at McDonald's that got pregnant at 14 can now go on the phone and take 80 hours to study, then graduate and get a dollar extra an hour. If she works 40 hours a week, that's $40 times 50 weeks. That's $2,000 more a year. The GED will fundamentally change her life.

Internationally, we are doing universal sign language with Kathy Buckley. Kathy Buckley is the funniest, brightest, most generous, kind-hearted deaf comedian who always works for me at my Soul Motion Ball. I raise a lot of money every year for these projects. If you want to come, just go to MarkVictorHansen.com and you can look at it. We've got cool videos and great invitations, and they sell out quickly.

Mark Victor Hansen

A Bengali will be able to do business with a Pakistani and they'll be able to do it with universal hand sign language, and that will all be up and running in a couple of months. Everyone said I couldn't do it. They were fearful because they were stupid. They're in dysfunctional models. When you get successful, you get out of being dysfunctional. You get out of being a bureaucrat. You get out of being a plebe. You get out of being a unionized mentality person. Everybody ought to be self-responsible, self-initiating, self-determining, self-generating, and then we'll get this stuff done.

It sounds like I'm a little pushy and dictatorial. It's just because we're having this breakdown of employment right now and people are losing their jobs. I've figured out how to get the economy going again. I don't think like normal people do. I *Think & Grow Rich*.

Do you have any parting words of advice for us?

For those of you listening to or reading my interview, if you get a chance, you ought to come to one of my seminars live. I'm not mono-maniacal about only mine; there are many phenomenal, great, and inspiring teachers out and about. Naomi just touches everybody's heart. Jim gets them to think about finances. You've got to hear the greats of our time. Bob Proctor, Michael Beckwith, Jack Canfield, Bob Allen, Cynthia Kersey, Crystal Dwyer. There's a ton of phenomenal talent out there that you need to hear. Each speaker polishes a different facet of your mind and makes you more radiant and able to shine.

Thank you so much for your time today.

You may reach Mark Victor Hansen at:
www.markvictorhansen.com

NOTES:

NOTES:

Chapter 2

WILLIAM ESTEB
Creative Director of Patient Media

"Once you see and understand how these principles work, there is no reason to go back to being oblivious."
-William Esteb

After a career in advertising and film production, Mr. Esteb was introduced to chiropractic in 1981 when he was asked to write the world's first patient education video, what became known as the Peter Graves video for Renaissance International.

Since then he has brought his "patient's-point-of-view" to many facets of chiropractic. He has conducted over 50 in-office consultation and patient focus groups that have provided fodder for 10 books, several of which are used as texts at various chiropractic colleges. He has traveled over 1.4 million miles sharing his unique perspective with chiropractors around the world.

Currently he serves as the creative director of Patient Media, Inc. (www.patientmedia.com) where he provides patient-relevant education and communication tools. He is also co-founder of Perfect Patients (www.perfectpatients.com) the interactive website service for chiropractors.

When he isn't *writing* about chiropractic or *speaking* about chiropractic, he can usually be found *thinking* about chiropractic—from a patient's point of view.

William Esteb

Notes from the editors:

I have had the privilege of a one-on-one lunch break with Mr. William Esteb after a seminar. From that insightful encounter, I found Mr. Esteb to be a purposeful and driven man with great vision.

> "Success is the ability to be proactive rather than reactive."
> –Dr. William Esteb

In the following interview, you will learn how Mr. Esteb applied Napoleon Hill's philosophy to grow his business, develop purpose, make keen decisions and cultivate faith. What is even most impressive is that Mr. Esteb had not yet read the book *Think and Grow Rich* when we approached him. What he encountered after reading the book was what he calls, "the DNA of success principles." In other words, he was living these principles and applying them without ever reading the philosophy. Mr. Esteb is not a chiropractor, but he thinks, acts, and looks like one! His message today for chiropractic is a critical one.

- Dr. Matt Hammett

Dr. Trish Hammett interviewing Mr. William Esteb.

Could you repeat what you just told me about how you were first introduced to this book?

Sure. I searched my library, which is extensive actually, for a copy of *Think and Grow Rich,* assuming that such a classic would be there, but it was not. Therefore, I searched and found a copy online and began reading it. I had not read the book before, but I recognized many of the principles because some mentors and people whom I respect had shared them with me. I had also seen some of the ideas in success literature that I have read over the years. In a sense, I suddenly uncovered the mother load, or the DNA, you might say, of some of the success principles that I think we take for granted. I certainly have. I read the book recently, but I have been familiar with the principles.

You mentioned that this was the "DNA of other success principles". Can you give us an overview as to how this philosophy as impacted your life?

There are many principles that I lifted right out of scripture, frankly, such what you set your heart on and the rich get richer, the poor get poorer from Matthew. Some of the other principles come from Proverbs. In some ways, this was not as much of a new collection as it was a distillation of other success literature. Those would probably be some of the biggest ones.

You are very well known in chiropractic, but for the one or two people who are not familiar with you and your work; could you tell us briefly about your background in chiropractic?

Well, not being a chiropractor myself, I have found a niche in helping chiropractors bridge the gap between what they know and what patients do not know. My focus has largely patient communications and, more specifically, patient education. I got my start back in 1981 when I was working for a film production company. From my involvement with this company, Drs. Guy Riekeman and Joseph Flesia of *Renaissance International* introduced me to chiropractic. They were in the process of getting ready to create patient education videos for the profession, which was quite an innovation back in the early 80's when we were still playing with Betamax and VHS. They invited our firm to help them create their videos by invited me to attend one of their seminars where I was 'really' introduced to chiropractic. I have to confess, I had a negative or a tainted view of chiropractic based on the cultural notions of chiropractic at the time. What I heard that weekend from those two inspiring leaders resonated with me. It made sense that the nervous system controlled everything.

I began chiropractic care literally as a research project to prepare for writing the patient education videos, so I started on a non-symptomatic basis. I saw the incredible need that chiropractors faced. They needed help to be able to explain their principles to people who, for the most part, were suffering from a cultural hypnosis of the allopathic medical model. That is what I have been doing for the last 27 years.

What highlights or accomplishments are you most proud of

William Esteb

in your personal and professional life?

In my personal life, I would say my 31-year marriage and my family. We have had three generations living under our roof at the same time, and the challenges that presents (as well as the incredible benefits) have been quite remarkable. I do not take that for granted a single day. Also on a personal level, I try to be as healthy as I can be, not as an idol but as a way of "walking the walk." If you are going to influence healthcare providers, you have to be healthy yourself, based on the law of the lid: the student rarely gets smarter than the teacher, and the patient rarely gets healthier than the doctor. I think just attending to those issues, not just physically but also mentally, intellectually, emotionally, and spiritually. It is more than just physical health.

On a professional level, the fact that I have started three successful businesses that have helped many chiropractors and patients has been an important milestone. I have also written ten books that describe the doctor-patient relationship from a patient's point of view. Gosh, I do not really spend a lot of time even thinking about that. I am sure there are other professional accomplishments I should mention. Being able to stand in front of a group of people and share my ideas, I suppose, is a professional accomplishment. I am the high school wallflower, the guy that would never raise his hand in class to offer an idea or suggestion. The fact that I am out there sharing ideas in front of a group of people, I suppose, would be both a personal and professional accomplishment.

In *Think & Grow Rich,* the publisher's preface says that 'riches cannot always be measured in money'. We would like to hear your thoughts on this statement and your own personal definition of being rich.

As I was reading this book recently, I saw that the Great Depression influenced Napoleon's (concept of being rich). Having money was a major focus of the book. He would probably be quick to point out that riches show up and affluence shows up in many, many other areas. I think there has been somewhat of a blurred notion that success and riches are the same. I have personally met many people who are quite rich financially, but who exhibit incredible poverty in other areas of their lives. One should want to be very careful about equating riches and success.

What is your definition of being successful?

The definition of success is based upon a certain aspect from which you are speaking. For example, physical success would have its bearing in terms of health, wellbeing, vitality, energy, and longevity. Financial success would be the sense of having affluent and abundant resources. Family success would be measured differently. It would be about how well you keep your I-love-you's current and what your relationship is with your parents, your siblings, your own children, and your spouse. Each one of those different disciplines, whether they be family, mental, spiritual, or financial has a different meaning of success.

It is important to have a sense of ease about those disciplines, whether in your spiritual life, your mental life or your family life, and to be able to have adequate resources in those areas so that you are not constrained. For example, one of the things very important to me when it comes to "success" is the ability to use my time as I see fit and not to be constrained to have to do something else.

In *Think & Grow Rich!*, Napoleon Hill includes the following quote:

"A peculiar thing about this secret of riches is that those who acquire it and use it find themselves literally swept on to success, but with little effort, and they never again submit to failure."

We would like to hear some more of your thoughts on that statement.

There is a parable in Matthew 25 that talks about the talents. In Matthew 25: "Unto everyone that hath shall be given, and he shall have abundance, but from him that hath not shall be taken even that which he hath." As I said earlier, the rich get richer and the poor get poorer. It has to do with understanding the principles that, like gravity, just cannot be broken. Once you see and understand how these principles work, there is no reason to go back to being oblivious. Once you lose a beginner's mind, it is very difficult to go back. That is partly what is at work here. Once you see it in action and once you see how these principles work when consistently applied, it is somewhat hard to go back.

William Esteb

Parable of the Talents

Matthew 25

"**1** Then shall the kingdom of heaven be like to ten virgins, who taking their lamps went out to meet the bridegroom and the bride. **2** And five of them were foolish and five wise. **3** But the five foolish, having taken their lamps, did not take oil with them. **4** But the wise took oil in their vessels with the lamps. **5** And the bridegroom tarrying, they all slumbered and slept. **6** And at midnight there was a cry made: Behold the bridegroom cometh. Go ye forth to meet him. **7** Then all those virgins arose and trimmed their lamps. **8** And the foolish said to the wise: Give us of your oil, for our lamps are gone out. **9** The wise answered, saying: Lest perhaps there be not enough for us and for you, go ye rather to them that sell and buy for yourselves. **10** Now whilst they went to buy the bridegroom came: and they that were ready went in with him to the marriage. And the door was shut. **11** But at last came also the other virgins, saying: Lord, Lord, open to us. **12** But he answering said: Amen I say to you, I know you not. **13** Watch ye therefore, because you know not the day nor the hour.**14** For even as a man going into a far country called his servants and delivered to them his goods; **15** And to one he gave five talents, and to another two, and to another one, to every one according to his proper ability: and immediately he took his journey. **16** And he that had received the five talents went his way and traded with the same and gained other five. **17** And in like manner he that had received the two gained other two. **18** But he that had received the one, going his way, digged into the earth and hid his lord's money. **19** But after a long time the lord of those servants came and reckoned with them. **20** And he that had received the five talents coming, brought other five talents, saying: Lord, thou didst deliver to me five talents. Behold I have gained other five over and above. **21** His lord said to him: Well done, good and faithful servant, because thou hast been faithful over a few things, I will place thee

Inspire Chiropractic

over many things. Enter thou into the joy of thy lord. **22** And he also that had received the two talents came and said: Lord, thou deliveredst two talents to me. Behold I have gained other two. **23** His lord said to him: Well done, good and faithful servant: because thou hast been faithful over a few things, I will place thee over many things. Enter thou into the joy of thy lord. **24** But he that had received the one talent, came and said: Lord, I know that thou art a hard man; thou reapest where thou hast not sown and gatherest where thou hast not strewed. **25** And being afraid, I went and hid thy talent in the earth. Behold here thou hast that which is thine. **26** And his lord answering, said to him: Wicked and slothful servant, thou knewest that I reap where I sow not and gather where I have not strewed. **27**Thou oughtest therefore to have committed my money to the bankers: and at my coming I should have received my own with usury. **28** Take ye away therefore the talent from him and give it him that hath ten talents. **29** For to every one that hath shall be given, and he shall abound: but from him that hath not, that also which he seemeth to have shall be taken away. **30** And the unprofitable servant, cast ye out into the exterior darkness. There shall be weeping and gnashing of teeth. **31** And when the Son of man shall come in his majesty, and all the angels with him, then shall he sit upon the seat of his majesty. **32** And all nations shall be gathered together before him: and he shall separate them one from another, as the shepherd separateth the sheep from the goats: **33** And he shall set the sheep on his right hand, but the goats on his left. **34** Then shall the king say to them that shall be on his right hand: Come, ye blessed of my Father, possess you the kingdom prepared for you from the foundation of the world. **35** For I was hungry, and you gave me to eat: I was thirsty, and you gave me to drink: I was a stranger, and you took me in: **36**Naked, and you covered me: sick, and you visited me: I was in prison, and you came to me. **37**Then shall the just answer him, saying: Lord, when did we see thee hungry and fed thee: thirsty and gave thee drink? **38** Or when did we see thee a stranger and took thee in? Or naked and covered thee? **39** Or when did we see thee sick or in prison and came to thee? **40** And the king answering shall say to them: Amen I say to you, as long as you did it to one of these my least brethren, you did it to me. **41** Then he shall say to them also that shall be on his left hand: Depart from me, you cursed, into everlasting fire, which was prepared for

William Esteb

the devil and his angels. **42** For I was hungry and you gave me not to eat: I was thirsty and you gave me not to drink. **43** I was a stranger and you took me not in: naked and you covered me not: sick and in prison and you did not visit me. **44** Then they also shall answer him, saying: Lord, when did we see thee hungry or thirsty or a stranger or naked or sick or in prison and did not minister to thee? **45** Then he shall answer them, saying: Amen: I say to you, as long as you did it not to one of these least, neither did you do it to me. **46** And these shall go into everlasting punishment: but the just, into life everlasting.'
The Douay-Rheims Bible

Do you feel that there is any such thing as failure in life, or are there only lessons to be learned?

There is such a thing as failure. When something does not work as if you imagined it is going to work, we would call that failure. However, culture has misrepresented failure and has denigrated it. When I look back on some of the richest lessons, I have learned and the life-shaping events I have experienced, an objective viewer would call them failures. In addition, granted, they might be. Nevertheless, I learned so much from them and they were such an important part of my own personal development that I believe you should not try to save someone from failure.

Certainly, in my early years as a parent, I succumbed to the notion that my role as a parent was to prevent my child from experiencing the slings and arrows of life. In the process of protecting someone, you can literally make someone afraid of the world because of the meanings that you attach to failure. This is all wrapped up in quite an extensive exploration that Napoleon Hill gives about the subject of fear.

I am not sure that failure is anti-success. I think there is the notion that failure is on one side of the coin and success is on the other. I do not see it that way. Failure is part of the process, and it is something that, frankly, should be celebrated. It is the meaning that we have attached to failure that gets in our way.

Are there any particular lessons you learned through those failures that you could share with us?

Inspire Chiropractic

The most fundamental failure I have had and the one that was the most devastating was shortly after I sold my old company and started Patient Media ten years ago. I made the tremendous mistake of thinking about me alone and making the company about me rather than about the customers, I wanted to serve. I had a rather egotistical experience for the first year or two, until the capital I was using from the sale of the old company began to decrease. Once it was exhausted, I was confronted with the prospect of not being able to pay my bills on time, which I had never experienced before. It was a powerful and profound wakeup call that inspired me to vow to make the business about our customers instead of about my name and me. The moment I turned the company over to the customers, I saw a huge uptake in the success of our company. Things turned around and moved forward. However, on that brink, when I was attempting to make the business about me rather than the customers, I almost smothered the company with my own ego.

I see this often and I am now able to recognize it in chiropractors who are going through a rough patch. Usually they make that rough patch about themselves rather than looking for ways to serve their customers better, or more completely, or coming up with new ways of serving. For me, it was a watershed event, and while very painful at that moment, I would not want that taken away from me.

> "The way one can be decisive is to know one's purpose, and I think to know one's purpose and to live it is on of our primary directives during our experience here on the planet."

That lesson, and many others like that, are very powerful and are part of the journey. You have to be able to put yourself behind and really show up as a humble servant. That is when we start brushing up against something we call success.

Napoleon Hill talks about the importance of a mastermind group. Could you share with us who would be in your ultimate mastermind group? This can be people that are living and dead.

I confess that I never really had a virtual mastermind group, although I am incredibly interested in the wisdom and the truth of

William Esteb

Jesus and I consult the scriptures daily. Probably as a practical matter in terms of business and other aspects of life, I probably would align more with Socrates. I am blessed with an incredible curiosity, which plays nicely into the Socratic Method. In fact, I would suggest that my ability to help licensed professionals is largely because I am incredibly inquisitive and want to know why and how things work. That curiosity has served me well.

However, in terms of bringing a group of these minds of the past together and kind of questioning them as Napoleon Hill describes is something that I have not done. Instead, I have tended to consult books. I am a voracious reader. I have probably six to eight people that I consult regularly that are both in the chiropractic profession and outside of it. I also have a blog where I am able to write some of my newest ideas and get feedback on them, which refines those ideas. I guess I have a mastermind group, but not in the way, Napoleon Hill has postulated it.

Napoleon Hill lists thirteen steps to riches: desire, faith, autosuggestion, specialized knowledge, imagination, organized planning, decision, persistence, power of the mastermind, the mystery of sex transmutation, the subconscious mind, the brain, and the sixth sense. Is there one of those steps that you feel is the most important?

There are two steps that I really resonate with and one that is most important. The two that I resonate with in particular are faith and decision. When you know your purpose, you are able to make decisions very quickly. You are able to say "no" more easily to off-purpose tangents, opportunity seeking, and some of the other things that get people off their task. It is literally like being attracted to shiny objects.

Faith is probably the superior one. It has to do with the mindset and the headspace of what you do between an action and the manifestation of your intent. If you are in the healing arts, you have to have a certain level of faith, but I think this is crucial when you are attempting to manifest a change in your life. As a culture, we tend to be wrapped up in the doing of something: "Tell me what to do. Show me what to do." In fact, it is really about being faithful. If you know who you are and you know what your purpose is, you do not need a list from someone else to tell you what to do, or even how to answer the phone, frankly. It is a matter of staying true to that and being faithful to the laws of the

Inspire Chiropractic

universe.

He goes on to say that before any of these steps can be put into practice, we must clear three enemies out of our minds: indecision, doubt, and fear. Could you share with us some tools that you have used to clear those enemies out of your way?

I confess I was the poster child for fear for a long time until I encountered an incredible healer named Scott Walker, who has discovered the neuro-emotional technique. As I studied this technique, I started learning about fear. I learned how fear worked from a physiological point of view. I have been receiving NET care since around 1995 or 1996, and that has been an immeasurable help for me in putting fear aside and allowing me to enjoy health on an entirely different level. I think many of the physical maladies that we face are literally unresolved emotional issues, and NET has been incredibly instrumental in making us aware of that.

The second tool that I have learned is EFT, which stands for emotional freedom technique. It is the work of Gary Craig and others, popularized by McCullough and others. Learning EFT has been helpful because sometimes you do not have a NET practitioner in your vicinity when you are facing some of these issues. EFT is something that is more self-administered, and it has shown to be quite helpful from time to time.

Probably the third and most powerful thing that I have been utilizing is intercessory prayer. Intercessory prayer is something I have learned through my chiropractic experience, since my current chiropractor has included that as part of the care regimen. That has just gone with many, many other breakthroughs.

Do you have any parting words of advice for us?

It is crucial that we know ourselves and that we know the truth. The truth will set us free, and as I have learned about myself and about my shortcomings and areas for improvement, I am aware of truths that have been uncomfortable, embarrassing, and maybe even shameful on occasion. All of that is crucial to knowing who you are. Self-development is one of our key responsibilities. I think that Napoleon Hill's book, classic that it is, still has incredible relevance today. It offers principles that have

William Esteb

stood the test of time. Hill's principles are included in virtually all of the success literature that has come since his work. To that, all of us owe a debt of gratitude.

You may reach William Esteb at:
(800) 486-2337

Chapter 3

DR. BOB HOFFMAN
President of *The Masters Circle*

"I was so engrossed by what was written and the principles that were taught that I have been following, studying, and teaching these principles ever since."
-Dr. Bob Hoffman

Dr. Bob Hoffman is the President and CEO of *The Masters Circle*, a highly specialized and unique Leadership Training and Practice Building organization that has revolutionized the traditional model of management consulting for chiropractors common in our profession today. In addition, he is a co-author of the best selling book, "Discover Wellness: How Staying Healthy Can Make You Rich."

Dr. Hoffman graduated from New York Chiropractic College in 1978. He is licensed in the state of New York and is Nationally Board Certified. He ran a very successful, cash-only, high volume practice on Long Island for twenty-two years before pursuing his dream of leading and guiding an unsurpassed group of chiropractic professionals with a multitude of college backgrounds, political affiliations, practice sizes and technique styles toward the lifestyle and practice of their dreams.

Throughout his distinguished career he has achieved a plethora of honors including being the 12th President of the International Chiropractors Association; a renowned organization which began

Dr. Bob Hoffman

in 1926 and participating as a Chairman for the Board of the New York Chiropractic Council.

As a well know figure in the profession, Dr. Hoffman accepts approximately thirty speaking engagements a year (worldwide) and has appeared on numerous radio and television shows. In addition, he currently writes articles for numerous monthly chiropractic publications that have a circulation of over hundreds of readers.

From the stage, Dr. Hoffman seems to "connect" on a very personal basis with his audiences. His passion for chiropractic shines through and his believability makes everyone present feel that they too can achieve long-lasting success and fulfillment.

> "When we're doing God's work, when we're fulfilling our life purpose, when we find great joy and satisfaction and fulfillment in what we do, for most people, especially when we do it with the right intent, for most people there is an effortless ease that the world just opens up to you."
> – Dr. Bob Hoffman

Dr. Hoffman has proudly produced over 16 Chiropractic products that have made an important and positive contribution in the profession and he is the author two national recognized newsletters, "Secrets to Creating the Practice of Your Dreams" and "Chiropractic Miracles." In addition, approximately 1500 DC's currently subscribe to his quarterly "Chiropractic Clipping Service", documenting the health care trends in society away from the allopathic drug model and toward the wellness/chiropractic model of health care.

Notes from the editors:

On many occasions, I have had the opportunity to attend seminars given by *The Master Circle*. I must say, that Dr. Hoffman is one of the most gifted and dynamic speakers I have ever heard. Take a moment and read this interview. I am sure you will find it to be exhilarating!

Dr Hoffman utilizes Napoleon Hill's principle, the power of the mastermind, very effectively. He explains how this principle has influenced both his professional and personal life. Dr. Hoffman calls this principle "modeling" or his "board of directors" and he credits his success in life to this teaching. He also describes a need to develop "an awakened, enlivened sense of awareness", which, of course, corresponds with Napoleon Hill's principle of "the sixth sense." In addition, you will discover some new tools from Dr. Hoffman that will help you become more decisive, or as Napoleon Hill put it: "a definitive of purpose."

-Dr. Matt Hammett

Dr. Trish Hammett interviewing Dr. Bob Hoffman:

Starting out, can you tell us how you were first introduced to Napoleon Hill's *Think & Grow Rich*?

In my very early 20s, when I was in chiropractic college, I was introduced to the whole genre of self-help personal growth books. One of the very first books I ever read was Napoleon Hill's book, *Think & Grow Rich*. As you research the subject of personal growth, you quickly discover that Napoleon Hill is one of the granddaddies of the entire self-help and personal growth movement. The book immediately and instantly resonated with me. I was so engrossed by what was written and the principles that were taught that I have been following, studying, and teaching these principles ever since.

Could you tell us specifically how some of those principles influenced your life?

I had never even heard of what self-help or personal growth was. It was an unknown subject to me. It was by diving into books like *Think & Grow Rich* that I received this passion to have a lifetime, lifelong commitment to self growth, and to understanding that who you are always determines how well what you do works. I studied many of the principles and I have applied many of the principles to my life, to my chiropractic practice and to running *The Masters Circle*; all of this with great success and with effortless ease.

Even things about the history of the book that were not talked about in the book have guided my life. For example, I am well

Dr. Bob Hoffman

aware of the fact that Napoleon Hill was commissioned by one of the most powerful men in the world at that time, Andrew Carnegie, to study the most successful people in the world at that time. This was because Carnegie believed that success was a formula, and that success left clues. He believed that once you learned the system of success, and the principles of success, it could be replicated and duplicated repeatedly.

> "Success, as I said, leaves clues and there was no reason to reinvent the wheel."

I have myself, throughout my entire adult professional career, spent as much time as I can getting to know, meet, listen to, and learn from other dignitaries in the chiropractic profession. This has included pioneers of the chiropractic profession, leaders of the chiropractic profession, as well as opinion leaders and leaders outside of the profession. I have done this so that I can become a better version of myself. Success, as I said, leaves clues and there was no reason to reinvent the wheel. So I have constantly looked to study what people do, how they think, how they act, how they handle adversity, how they work on themselves, how they make their own life a priority, how they live a life of purpose. Then I have tried to emulate that as best I can.

Can you tell us briefly about your background in chiropractic?

When I was a freshman in college, I had gotten ill. Nobody really knew what was wrong with me. I went to a medical doctor, had blood work done and found out that I had a very advanced case of mononucleosis. The doctor told me that I would be quarantined for three to five months, no visitors. Now, when you are 18 or 19 years old, three to five months is just short of a lifetime. The day the blood work came back my mom went to the monthly meeting of an organization and the guest speaker was a chiropractor. She went up and asked him about mono and chiropractic. Long story short, that evening I ended up in his office. I had never even heard of a chiropractor before that, so he explained it to me. He sat down with me and explained what chiropractic was, what mononucleosis was and why he was certain he could help me get well. I agreed to proceed. He took an x-ray of my spine that looked like a roadmap. I had no clue

Inspire Chiropractic

that my spine was so twisted and bent. He proceeded to adjust me, and I broke out into an intense sweat. That night I slept 12 hours; I do not know if I had slept 12 hours combined in the week before. I woke up in the morning and I felt significantly different and better, still not completely better but there was a marked improvement. I went back to the chiropractor every other day. At the end of the week, I was about 90% back to feeling like my old self. At the end of two weeks, the chiropractor insisted that I go back to the doctor and have a set of blood work done. I did, and the doctor said to me that he must have made a misdiagnosis because he had never seen ever mononucleosis clear up in two weeks.

I was so moved and so grateful that every Friday when I did not have school, I used to go this chiropractor's office and just sit in his reception room. I would interview his patients and ask questions. I would see people limp in and walk out, coming in crying and going out laughing. The more I observed and the more I learned and the more questions I asked and got answers to, the more I knew that this was a direction my life should go in. Therefore, I started taking all my pre-requirements and went to chiropractic school.

In *Think & Grow Rich*, the publisher's preface says that riches cannot always be measured in money. We would like to hear your thoughts on that statement and your own personal definition of what it means to be rich.

First, I agree with the preface that riches cannot always be measured in money. Oftentimes it is never measured in money. Riches is the richness of your life, the richness of your relationships, the richness of your spirituality, your connection with your own inner voice and your innate voice, your family, your friends, and living your life's purpose. All of those things, and many others, add to the beauty, the joy, the fulfillment, and the richness of our lives. Now, for many people, although not all, when you are living your life in gratitude, feeling blessed, and living your life's work and are supported by a loving family, it usually does manifest into materialistic wealth as well. However, of all that, wealth is probably the least important.

Do you feel that being rich and being successful is the same thing?

Not necessarily, In answering your question more clearly, since

Dr. Bob Hoffman

most people in our world equate rich and successful, there are plenty of people who are very, very successful in life, but not necessarily so monetarily. There are some that are blessed with both. There are some people who are rich monetarily, who are not leading a successful life, or a life that they are proud. We have proven that all the time with celebrities, athletes, performers, and entertainers who are worth millions, but who are on either alcohol or drugs or commit suicide because they live a hollow, unhappy life. Therefore, these are two separate things that are at times connected. There are some blessed people that are experiencing both simultaneously and, as a result, I think many people associate one with the other and they are not.

Napoleon Hill says, "a peculiar thing about this secret of riches is that those who once acquire it and use it find themselves literally swept on to success, but with little effort and they never again submit to failure." We would like to hear your thoughts on that statement.

Well, one of the things that we talk about in *The Masters Circle* is this issue of effortless ease. I think that is completely related to this quote. When we're doing God's work, when we're fulfilling our life purpose, when we find great joy and satisfaction and fulfillment in what we do, for most people, especially when we do it with the right intent, for most people there is an effortless ease that the world just opens up to you. The world shares its riches back with you.

Another principle that we teach in *The Masters Circle* is the principle of circle-circle, which states what goes around comes around. What you put out to the universe comes back to you. So when you're doing good things, when you're doing good work, when you're doing the masters work, when you're serving for the sake of serving and loving unconditionally, more often than not—there's no exact guaranteed formula—but more often than not, what comes back into your life is a blessing. When we are loving to other people, people tend to be loving to us. When we share our wealth and wisdom and knowledge with people, other people tend to share their wealth, wisdom, and knowledge with us. When we pay our bills on time, other people pay our bill on time. When we have great intent to help others, others have great intent to help us. That is what is meant by circle-circle and I think clearly what Napoleon Hill meant by that principle.

Do you believe there is any such thing as failures in life?

Inspire Chiropractic

Society would obviously like us to think that; that there are haves and have not's, the successful and the unsuccessful, and the upper class and the lower class. Nevertheless, the truth is that there is no such thing as failure. There are lessons that we are constantly learning. If we learn them, we move on to the next lesson. If we fail to learn them, that lesson is repeated over and over again. Therefore, there really is no such thing as failure. There are missed opportunities and learning opportunities.

Can you share with us some of the learning opportunities you have encountered?

As a chiropractor, there are times that I have adjusted patients in a certain way and they were not responding, but I thought I was doing it the right way because my ego was involved. I got to the point of becoming more humble and realizing that if what I was doing wasn't working, perhaps I should try a different approach to adjusting them; adjusting them either harder or softer or a different procedure and technique and analysis. I could honestly say that probably 99 out of 100 times the patient then did respond. So part of the issue here with your question, part of the answer is that one must have an awakened, enlivened sense of awareness so that you can make distinctions and can learn lessons so that you can adapt and make the changes necessary to succeed at a higher rate next time.

Napoleon Hill talked about the importance of a mastermind group. If you could put together your ideal mastermind group out of people both living and dead, who would be in your group?

What a great question. You know, years ago, I created in my own mind my board of directors. I actually visualized whom I was sitting next to and who was next to that person, etc. I would meditate frequently with my board of directors and ask questions. Boy, that really helped me tremendously growing as a person and as a professional. Therefore, my board of directors was the same thing as masterminds for me. A mastermind is whenever people of like mind come together to create a greater consciousness, a greater good. Who I would include on that mastermind are people like Walt Disney, people like Oprah Winfrey, people like Mother Teresa, people like George Burns, because I love humor, people like Donald Trump. I would include people like B.J. Palmer, Mahatma Gandhi, and the Dali

Dr. Bob Hoffman

Lama. The list is basically endless. It is looking for those qualities, characteristics, and traits that you most admire and what people in the world currently or in the past exhibit or exhibited the highest level of those traits. For example, Walt Disney for me would exhibit the trait of innovation. I value that very much. Mother Teresa had unconditional love. I value that quality very much. So I think who is in your world class mastermind is different for each one of us, depending upon those qualities, characteristics, and traits that we most admire or we consider weaknesses in our life and we're looking for a place to gain strength from.

Can you also share with us some of your favorite books and authors and the reasons you believe these books are worthy of us getting to know?

Wow. You know, as a result of reading Napoleon Hill's book thirty some-odd years ago, I've probably been reading on average about two books a month for the last thirty some-odd years. Therefore, there are many books that I can give to you. I think for me it breaks down, again, by whom I resonate with. I really love John Maxwell's books on leadership. I love Robin Sharma, I feel like he is speaking to me. I love Malcolm Gladwell's books. In fact, I just finished his newest book, *Outlier*, which I thought was sensational. I really love Michael Gerber's books, so I can become a better businessperson. There are so many to choose from. I have always loved reading Deepak Chopra's work. I love a lot of the work that came out of the Gallup Organization, *Breakthrough Company*, *Good to Great*. There are so many books that one can put into this category. *Power vs. Force*, David Hawkins. It is endless, quite frankly. It is endless the quality of material that's out in the marketplace and what we can learn and gain from it, which is one of the reasons I'm a book-a-holic.

Going back to *Think & Grow Rich*, Napoleon Hill talks about thirteen steps to riches. He talks about desire, faith, autosuggestion, specialized knowledge, imagination, organized planning, decision, persistence, power of the mastermind, the mystery of sex trans-mutation, the subconscious mind, the brain, and the sixth sense. Of these steps, which are a few of your favorite principles and why?

First, all of the above, obviously, because I think that is a terrific

Inspire Chiropractic

list. One of the things that we in The Masters Circle have taught for a long time, I personally believe with every fiber of my being, is that the first rule of success is decisiveness. One must make a decision. We live in such a fast-paced world that I do not think we even have the luxury of making decisions slowly anymore. We have to make a decision and then do whatever is necessary to make it the right decision. I think persistence is critical. So many people in today's world are excellent at starting things, but not finishing.

> "Darkness is nothing but the absence of the presence of light."

So many chiropractors that we know have what has been referred to over the years as a yo-yo or roller coaster type practice. They do all the little things that are necessary to grow their business. As they get busier and busier, they stop doing all those little things that are so necessary and slowly the practice starts to drift and drop again. They get to a certain threshold—and everybody has a different threshold—where they get so upset, so frustrated or so desperate that they start to go back to doing all those little, basic, important, necessary things all over again and it grows. That cycle continues throughout a career, unless someone is fortunate enough to have someone who, as a confidant, a friend, or mentor, or coach, point that out to them so that they can become more persistent. Consistent, persistent action always rules the day.

I think organized action is a critical quality. We have to be organized. There are priorities in our life. This gets back to the 20-80 principle. 80% of what we accomplish in life comes from 20% of our activities. 20% of the vertebra we adjust create 80% of our results. 20% of the hours we work produces 80% of the results in our life. We can take this principle and go on and on with it. So what are those 20% most important action items? It is different for every one of us, but in order to get to that conclusion, to make yourself far more efficient, far more productive, is you have to have organized actions. Again, this gets back to one of the points we made earlier, that you have to increase your level of awareness to notice the things that are most important and am I organized. Am I doing the highest priority items first instead of hoping to get to them at the end of the day?

Even within the concept of organized actions, I think we live in an

Dr. Bob Hoffman

energy universe. Every one of us, if we pay attention, we have far more energy at certain times of the day. Well, I try to attack my most important, highest priority, greatest return activities when I am at my peak self. That is part of organized action as well.

He goes on to say that before we can put any of those steps into practice that we have to clear three enemies out of our mind and he lists those as being indecision, doubt, and fear. Can you share with us some tools you have used to clear these enemies out of your way?

Well, part of it is a mindset. Part of it is a belief. Part of it is just getting leverage over yourself. There have been many times in my maturation that I was far more indecisive than I am today. I have had to train myself to become decisive. As I stated earlier, I try to make quick and terrific decisions and then I do whatever I have to do to try to make them the right decisions. I do not think there is anyone around that does not occasionally have doubt. Did I do the right thing? Did I say the right thing? Did I adjust the right area? Doubt is not our friend. It has never been our friend. We have to have enough faith, confidence, and belief in who we are and what we do, as well as faith, confidence, and belief in the universe being a good universe and things happening for a reason and recognize that doubt has never, ever created anything good in our life. That over time—it doesn't happen in one minute—but over time you get to become less doubting by becoming more confident.

Fear, again, this is something that we are born with certain fears. We certainly develop far more fears. Unfortunately, many people in today's world live in fear. Well, I believe just like light and darkness cannot coexist... There is no such thing as darkness. Darkness is nothing but the absence of the presence of light. If we were to extend that out further, there is really no such thing as sickness because sickness and health cannot coexist at the same time. Sickness is just the absence of the presence of health in the human spirit and the human body. I believe if we extend that one step further, you cannot have fear and faith coexist at the same time. I work on strengthening my faith, my beliefs, my trust, my confidence, my self-esteem every single day so that I have less and less fear.

Do you have any parting words of advice for us?

Inspire Chiropractic

My parting word of advice is I would urge anybody who I can influence to read a book like *Think & Grow Rich*, to learn what the masters before us learned, because success leaves clues and there's so much to learn from them. I would urge anyone who gets to read these words or to hear my voice to become a reader and to commit themselves to a life of personal improvement, to decide that improving oneself is really part, if not a major part, of our life's work and our life's purpose.

I still have a rather lengthy list of areas of my life that I believe are weaknesses that I need to turn into strengths. However, my list is dramatically shorter than it was a year or five years ago and probably unrecognizable to what it was ten or twenty years ago. I do not believe that I have any special qualities, characteristics, or traits that other people do not possess. I believe I have succeeded at the level I have succeeded because I have worked on improving myself every single day. There are some days that I work on improving myself for just a few moments and some days it is for a few hours and some days it is the whole day. In addition, there are many different ways to improve ourselves. Writing in your success journal, speaking to a mentor or friend or coach, someone who you can trust. It is reading a great book or listening to an audiotape or watching an empowering video. There are many, many ways to have personal growth, but you want to build your growth muscles. You want to constantly work on building that muscle by working it and working it and working it. In addition, when you do, the rewards are magnificent.

Thank you so, so much.

You may reach Dr. Bob Hoffman at:

The Masters Circle, Inc.
100 Jericho Quadrangle, Suite 140
Jericho, New York 11753
1-800-451-4514
bob@themasterscircle.com
www.themasterscircle.com

Dr. Bob Hoffman

NOTES:

Chapter 4

DR. FABRIZIO MANCINI
President of Parker College of Chiropractic
&
Parker Seminars

"This helped me to focus on the thoughts and behaviors that would allow me to attract wealth and richness into my life."
-Dr. Fabrizio Mancini

Dr. Fabrizio Mancini is an internationally-acclaimed speaker, author, educator and president of one of the leading chiropractic colleges in the U.S., Parker College of Chiropractic, located in Dallas, Texas.

An alumni of Parker College, Dr. Mancini took the helm in 1999 as the successor to his mentor, the late chiropractic pioneer Dr. James Parker. As such, Dr. Mancini became one of the youngest college presidents (age 33) in the U.S. Under his leadership, Parker College has grown exponentially and Parker Seminars, seminars tailored specifically to the chiropractic profession and its necessary accreditations, have become the largest chiropractic/wellness seminars in the world.

Dr. Fabrizio Mancini

Dr. Mancini has given testimony to the White House Commission for Complimentary and Alternative Medicine and has served for years on the Governor's Advisory Council on Physical Fitness. In 2003, Dr. Mancini co-authored, *Chicken Soup for the Chiropractic Soul*, and will soon publish, *Feeling Fab! A Wellness Approach to Successful Living.*

He is a fellow of the International College of Chiropractors, American College of Chiropractors and International Chiropractic Association and was recently inducted into the Wellness Revolutionaries Hall of Fame for his contributions in this field.

Dr. Mancini came to the United States with his family in 1978 from Colombia, South America with the dream to become a doctor. While studying pre-med at the University of Dallas, he discovered Parker College of Chiropractic and found his passion, to become a Doctor of Chiropractic. He graduated from Parker College in 1990 and opened practices in Miami and abroad, later returning to the Dallas area and establishing a practice there. During that time, he also served as Director of Admissions and Assistant to the President at Parker College. Dr. Mancini resides in Irving with his wife, Alicia, and two sons, Gianni and Luciano.

> "When I read the book, I recognized that I did have the essence of what allows you to attract richness into your life. The book allowed me to have a paradigm shift that was revolutionary."
> –Dr. Fabrizio Mancini

Notes **from the editors:**

Visualize entering into the mind of this legend in chiropractic. Imagine what he must have felt when, he heard the *Think and Grow Rich* philosophies as a student at the largest chiropractic convention centers in the world. Did these precepts give him the insight to become the next President of Parker College of Chiropractic and a visionary for the Parker Seminars? Did these teachings expand his view of his future at that time? Did these principles encourage this doctor to become a great healer,

Inspire Chiropractic

leader, visionary, and entrepreneur who would *shape* the profession of chiropractic forever?

How dare I offer the expression that Napoleon Hill *branded* chiropractic? On the other hand, do I have good reason? Read and find out!

-Dr. Matt Hammett

Dr. Trish Hammett interviewing Dr. Fabrizio Mancini:

How and when were you first introduced to Napoleon Hill's Think & Grow Rich?

The first time I was introduced to *Think & Grow Rich* was at a Parker seminar. In fact, it was my first Parker seminar. Dr. James W. Parker mentioned that this was one of the most influential books he had ever read regarding the idea of becoming rich or becoming wealthy.

Can you give us an overview of how this book and its philosophies have impacted your life?

When I first started reading this book, I was a student at Parker College of Chiropractic. During this time, I did not have a lot of material wealth due to the fact I was borrowing money to go to school. When I read the book, I recognized that I did have the essence of what allows you to attract richness into your life. The book allowed me to have a paradigm shift that was revolutionary. I learned that just because wealth had not manifested yet in material things, that did not mean I was not worthy of it. This helped me to focus on the thoughts and behaviors that would allow me to attract wealth and richness into my life. It gave me the tools I needed and the compass so I too may become one of the richest men in the world.

You are obviously very well known in chiropractic. For the one or two people who may not be familiar with you, can you tell us a little bit about your background in chiropractic?

I was born in Colombia, South America and came to live in the United States at the age of 13. I was a pre-med student studying to be a neurosurgeon when I was introduced to chiropractic by an orthopedic surgeon at the hospital where I was taken after a

Dr. Fabrizio Mancini

bad car accident. He referred me to his doctor of chiropractic, and after that experience, my life changed. I felt better not only physically, but also mentally, emotionally, and spiritually. I then interviewed about 60 chiropractors and decided after six months of research that I wanted to choose chiropractic rather than traditional medicine as my career. I enrolled in Parker College September of 1987, and graduated in August 1990.

I then went and associated with one of the most successful chiropractors in Miami, Florida. I learned many things from him and began to do a daily radio show. After six months of that, I was invited to work in the largest chiropractic clinic in Europe at the time. I was the sole practitioner taking care of hundreds of people every day. I did that for a year. Then I came back to the United States and was ready to pioneer chiropractic in Colombia. Dr. Parker, my mentor, talked me into working with him as his assistant to the president and director of admissions, which I did for two-and-a-half years.

Then, I had a dream of going back and starting my own practice here in Irving, Texas in December 1993. I accepted the position of the new Parker College of Chiropractic on June 7 1999. In December of 1999, I sold my practice to an alumnus due to the demand of this role.

What is your definition of being rich? In *Think & Grow Rich*, the publisher's preface says that riches cannot always be measured in money. We would like to hear your thoughts on that statement and then your own personal definition of what it means to be rich.

I was very fortunate to be raised by parents who had come from families that were wealthy. The way my parents raised us was with an understanding that it was not the materials you owned, but what you did for others that mattered. I grew up with that type of philosophy as a small child. Napoleon emphasizes this idea strongly in his book.

Inspire Chiropractic

> "The formula that I believe in and that Napoleon Hill found in his interviews, is that we first start with an idea of what it is we want to BE. Then we begin to DO the things that are required to attract what we want to HAVE."

As I have gotten older, I have recognized that the greatest treasures are our relationships. I usually put that on my Christmas card every year. I truly believe that if we only had 24 hours to live, very few of us would spend those 24 hours trying to earn more money. We would all spend that time truly appreciating, acknowledging, and celebrating those relationships that are meaningful to us. Understanding and making the things that matter a priority will attract a balanced wealthy life.

Do you feel that being rich and successful is the same thing?

Being rich tends to be more about attracting material wealth into your life. I define success more on the basis of achieving one's potential with every decision, person, event, circumstance, etc. I experience success on three different planes; Physical, Mental and Spiritual and in seven areas that I value most in my life- health, faith, family, relationships, career, finance and philanthropy. I feel that we all have a potential that is greater in all of these areas. The key is that we work in all of these areas every day of our lives. We also need to learn to discipline ourselves so that one area does not get us out of balance. Being financially rich does not guarantee that you will be happy, or loved. My father use to say, "Money makes you more of what you already are". So do not think money will ever be the answer of what defines you. I mentioned all the other things before that does.

In *Think & Grow Rich*, Napoleon Hill includes the following quote: "A peculiar thing about this secret of riches is that those who acquire it and use it find themselves literally swept on to success, but with little effort, and they never again submit to failure." We would like to hear your thoughts on that statement.

After reading that quote, I was able to recognize a formula of

Dr. Fabrizio Mancini

success called the "be, do, have." Unfortunately, most of us are conditioned to think that we first must have before we can do, and then we can be somebody. The formula that I believe in and that Napoleon Hill found in his interviews, is that we first start with an idea of what it is we want to BE. Then we begin to DO the things that are required to attract what we want to HAVE. Even when we have not attained the being completely, we begin to feel like perhaps it is possible and we begin to be a little bit more optimistic. That feeling is what attracts everything to us. When you live your life with that mindset, it allows you to recognize why success is effortless: it is because we got it backwards. Most people are so worried about the "having" that they forget the most important thing: what it is we want to be. When we start with the being, the rest is effortless because that is the core that will allow the law of attraction to be exercised. Everything will be attracted to us from the being.

Do you believe that there is any such thing as failures in life, or are they just lessons to be learned?

As a young person, there have been times that I have felt failure. When I was a kicker on my football team and I missed a kick, it was a failure. When I studied really hard to get a good grade in a class and got a C, that was a failure. However, later on in life I started recognizing that experiences are lessons to be learned. That idea became especially clear after reading this book. When Mr. Ford related how many times and how many tries it took to make something work, I was inspired. Now I have reached a point in my life where do not look at any experience as a failure. I look at it as an opportunity to reflect upon what I could do better in order to yield a greater result. It is so empowering to me to recognize that what defines me is not the outcome that I have experienced, but what I do with that experience that allows me to become better in the future.

Could you share with us some of the "failures" you have encountered in your journey through life and what lessons they taught you?

In high school, I was a very good student. My history professor also happened to be one of my football coaches. I strongly admired and looked up to him. In my history final exam, I did not know the answers to two out of 100 questions. Because I was young and immature and I wanted to make 100 on the test, I copied that person in front of me. My teacher saw me, pulled my

Inspire Chiropractic

test, and asked me to see him after class. He recognized that I had cheated and he wanted me to understand what I had done. He told me he would let me know on Monday what my punishment would be. That weekend was one of the toughest weekends in my life. I had nuts in my stomach and could not sleep. I recognized I had cheated myself and I had greatly disappointed someone I admired respected.

I got a zero for my final, which of course lowered my GPA. At the same time, my mentor taught me that you can spend a long time building respect and trust in a relationship, but it can all go away through one action. I also learned that I could earn that respect back over time, which I did. It was one of my greatest experiences, because now I avoid every temptation to do the wrong thing. That lesson always guides me back to the right path. I do not ever look as experiences as failures, but as blessings.

Thanks for sharing that. Napoleon Hill talks about the importance of a mastermind group. Could you share with us some people you would have in your ultimate mastermind group, both living and dead?

It is funny that you mention that, because I do believe in masterminding a great deal. When I read Napoleon's book, it was the first time I actually heard the term. I did not act upon his advice until maybe a year or two later. I was still in chiropractic school and there was a mastermind group of chiropractors that got together every Monday night in a restaurant. We would share ideas about what was working, and what was not working. I realized that even though I was still just a student, I was bringing a tremendous amount of passion to the doctors I was masterminding with. They had been in practice for a long time and were very successful, but sometimes they had lost a little bit of that passion of trying to impact the world.

Dr. Fabrizio Mancini

I found that mastermind groups are excellent. It is always an exchange. There is always somebody who needs something that the other person has, or there is always something that the other person has that can really make a difference in your life.

As a student some of the people in were successful chiropractors then as I started my practice, I also started masterminding with leaders in my community, church, mayors, senators, congress people, and very successful businesspeople. Now I find myself masterminding with transformational leaders. That is the group that I belong to right now. We mastermind ways we can contribute to humanity and create the kind of humanity that people can be very proud of, the kind that can be balance, prosperous and constructive.

In *Think & Grow Rich* Napoleon Hill lists thirteen steps to riches: desire, faith, autosuggestion, specialized knowledge, imagination, organized planning, decision, persistence, power of the mastermind, mystery of sex trans-mutation, the subconscious mind, the brain, and the sixth sense. Of these steps, which are a few of your favorite principles and why?

> "Faith is one of the critical ones because faith allows us to trust in what we cannot see, what we cannot control, and what is not in the physical realm."

Faith is one of the critical ones because faith allows us to trust in what we cannot see, what we cannot control, and what is not in the physical realm. During times of economic problems, faith really comes in. We need to recognize that we have some very bright people in the world, and we have some great leaders. We have to remember there have been difficult times throughout history, but we have always made it through, and we have always been better off after we experience those difficult times. Faith allows us to recognize that even though something has not happened the way we wanted, or even though we may be experiencing something very difficult, we must trust that there is a better tomorrow. We must have faith that it will be resolved. We must have faith that we will be stronger and better off once

Inspire Chiropractic

we conquer our difficulties.

Imagination is also very important to me. I have done a lot of mentoring in my life, especially with kids between the ages of 5 and 15. When you talk to children, you find a lot of imagination. When you play with a child, often you do not need fancy toys because they will come up with little games and toys that are practical and very inexpensive, but very entertaining. Unfortunately, people do not practice imagination on a day-to-day basis. They are not taking the time to dream and create that idea of what they would like to become, what they would like to attract, and what they would like to contribute. They are spending the majority of their time on survival. They are only doing what they can to barely make it. They just barely make it through their jobs and their lives. They spend most of their time dwelling in problems than focusing in solutions.

"This book taught me to recognize that the true purpose of wealth and riches is to dedicate our lives to the service of others. To search for the needs in the world and somehow find solutions that will help resolve them. When we dedicate our lives towards the service of others, is when we achieve the greatest amount of wealth and

Hill also says we must clear three enemies out of our minds: indecision, doubt, and fear. Could you share with us some tools that you have used to clear those enemies out of your mind?

I have to tell you, there is nothing worse than indecision. You often hear mentioned how a journey of a thousand steps, begins with a first step. Well, the first step is always the hardest one to take. Many times, we hesitate. I am very quick in making decisions because I recognize that once you exercise your judgment and you learn to make decisions, it is easy for you to make them and typically be right. Are all your decisions going to be right? Of course not. However, most likely, most of them are going to be right, and you will learn from the ones that did not too. Just practice making decisions and do not hesitate. Eventually, you will get really good at it.

Doubt prevents us from attracting the riches that Napoleon

Dr. Fabrizio Mancini

talked about because doubt arises when you focus on the probability of something not working rather than the possibility of something being greater than you ever thought it would be. The best way to deal with doubt is to focus on the positive rather than the negative. Focus on the possibilities rather than the probabilities. The biggest creators of doubt are the people around us because they are the ones that do not see what we see. They are the ones that do not experience what we experience. They do not believe in what we are doing as much as we do.

My greatest tool towards combating fear has been gratitude. When we live in gratitude, we constantly appreciate the present rather than being fearful of what may happen in the future. When you develop fear, you are always thinking more about the future than the present. Gratitude allows me to stay centered on what I have today and be thankful for that, rather than being focusing on what I may or may not have in the future, or what may or may not happen. We have to truly appreciate what we have today.

Do you have any parting words of advice for us?

This book taught me to recognize that the true purpose of wealth and riches is to dedicate our lives to the service of others. To search for the needs in the world and somehow find solutions that will help resolve them. When we dedicate our lives towards the service of others, is when we achieve the greatest amount of wealth and success.

Thank you.

You may reach Dr. Fabrizio Mancini at:
www.parkercc.edu

Inspire Chiropractic

NOTES:

Chapter 5

DR. JANICE HUGHES
Chiropractic coach and author

"Rich is family, rich is all the other aspects of your life that can bring you wealth without connecting to dollars."
-Dr. Janice Hughes

Dr. Janice Hughes is a life coach, healer (Chiropractor), published author, teacher and international speaker. She is an expert on matters of success, prosperity, abundance, wellness, and attraction. Dr. Hughes will assist and inspire you in transforming your life or your business by teaching you how to bring these concepts into your experience through simple and specific action steps. She is an experienced and proven transformational specialist, focused on evolving you and your business by putting the law of attraction into real action. She will be a catalyst for your inspiration by moving you into action!

> "Once we understand the concept of abundance and attraction, we attract everything into our lives: people, places, and things."
> – Dr. Janice

Notes from the editors:

I can still remember when Dr. Janice Hughes first came to Palmer College of Chiropractic. I was in my first year of chiropractic college at the time and many of the students were extremely excited to learn that Dr. Hughes would be teaching at Palmer. In fact, she was one of the most popular additions to Palmer while I attended. She is especially appreciated for her ability to teach transforming techniques that utilize the Law of Attraction. Grab your pen and learn from Dr. Janice Hughes.

-Dr. Matt Hammett

Dr. Trish Hammett interviewing Dr. Janice Hughes:

Tell us about you background in chiropractic.

I actually went into chiropractic after shifting away from the medical field. I have a microbiology degree, and I was doing a masters in microbiology and immunology. During that time, my dad went to a chiropractor and took my sister for migraine headaches. I was off at a university so I wasn't really connected with that, but then I got hurt and my dad referred me to his chiropractor.

My chiropractor never told me what inspired him to enter the field, but after I told him my educational background, he asked me, "With your background and degrees, you'd be a good chiropractor. Have you ever considered it?"

A light bulb turned on in my head. At the time, I was doing cancer research, and I wasn't loving it. Already I had started making a shift to more natural medicine. I decided to trust my intuition and investigate chiropractic further. I was accepted to the school in Canada, the Toronto school, which was the only chiropractic college at the time. I have trusted my intuition ever

Dr. Janice Hughes

since.

Do you practice on your own? I know you have been involved with *The Master Circle*.

I practiced in Brantford, Ontario. That was Wayne Gretsky's hometown. I was an associate there for just over 2 years before I went into practice on my own and ran what I would call a very philosophical practice. After working with a lot of kids, I began specializing in kids and families. My practice soon became family oriented. Then I got involved in Canadian politics and I did some political work in favor of chiropractic. I became the vice president of the Ontario Chiropractic Association.

By then I had three kids, and with them, the politics, and the traveling, I decided I needed a break. I left politics. While I was taking some time off from politics, I did some training as a certified coach through Coach University.

"When I first read the book, I tore through it, and then I quickly reread it. The book totally influenced my entire career and me as a coach."

After training to be a personal and professional coach, I began to speak and teach a lot more. I transitioned out of practice after grooming one of my associates to purchase my practice and take over.

Guy Reikman, a good friend of mine, had me come down and coach senior students at Palmer College from a business perspective. After that, Larry Markson had me come and speak. I was a guest speaker at one of their *The Masters Circle* series and Larry, Bob, and Dennis had asked me to do some coaching for them. I did some part time coaching while I was still at Palmer.

After I left Palmer, my husband and I decided to become U.S. based so I could do full time coaching with *The Masters Circle*. We moved to Boulder, Colorado where my husband reestablished a new practice. He really changed his niche. He now works with a lot of professional athletes, particularly cyclists. I am not actually licensed as a practicing chiropractor in the United States, so I did not practice at all. Instead, I spent 5 years full time coaching for *The Masters Circle*. I spoke and taught for them, then this past summer I left TMC (*The Masters Circle*) and

Inspire Chiropractic

have been doing some peer chiropractic coaching. Recently I have been involved in coaching and doing some contract work with Dr. Joan Fallon and her biotech company, *Curemark LLC*.

How and when were you first introduced to *Think and Grow Rich*?

I was actually handed a copy of *Think and Grow Rich* when I was in high school and ignored it. Then when I was in chiropractic, a wonderful practicing chiropractor that I had met through a couple of seminars gave me a copy of *Think and Grow Rich*. I first read it about halfway through my chiropractic training.

How did this book and its philosophies impact your life?

When I first read the book, I tore through it, and then I quickly reread it. The book totally influenced my entire career and me as a coach.

In *Think and Grow Rich*, the publisher's preface states, "Riches can not always be measured in money." We would like to hear thoughts on this statement and what your personal definition of rich is.

The statement defines everything that matters to me. Wealth has nothing to do with money. In the business world, people assume that money equals riches, but they need to redefine what success really means to them. It is based on values and living a value centered life. Rich is family, rich is all the other aspects of your life that can bring you wealth without connecting to dollars.

Do you feel that being rich and being successful is the same thing?

Not at all. I think that every human being comes to a point where they have to define what success means to them personally. One thing I do as a coach is teach about belief systems. Our belief systems are usually created by the time we are six years old, so our beliefs are often based on what everyone around us believes. Our definitions of success, money, wealth, or whatever word you use to describe it, actually come from other people. A lot of coaching involves pulling out those words and defining what they mean. What does the word "wealth" mean to each individual? What does the word "money" mean? What are your beliefs about money and what does success mean? Personally, I

Dr. Janice Hughes

think a lot of people I see realize that money fits in with their definition of success, but it is not the whole definition.

Do you have a personal motto for success?

I do: Success is about creating abundance and balance in all aspects of life.

What are some of your highest accomplishments in your life, both personally and professionally?

My highest accomplishment is having a phenomenal family. I have a significant other who loves and understands chiropractic as much as I do, which allows us to share certain values that are based on a strong philosophical perspective.

My next big accomplishment is clearly understanding my purpose, which is to inspire. I am able to work to live that purpose every day. I live it in my family by inspiring my kids to be who they are and everything they can be. I also live my purpose professionally. A huge accomplishment for me was running a phenomenal practice. I was a masterful chiropractor. I had some great mentors in my life, so a real accomplishment was being coachable and listening to some strong people, including the other people you are interviewing. They have been not only great mentors for me, but several of them are now my dearest friends. I also consider it an accomplishment to move into having those kinds of people in my life. They influence everything that I say and do.

In *Think and Grow Rich*, Napoleon Hill said, "A peculiar thing about the secret of riches is that those who once acquire and use it find themselves literally swept on to success, but with little effort, and they never again submit to failure." We would like to hear your thoughts on that statement.

That has to do with what I call attractability. Abundance and attractability. One of the things I've done a lot of in chiropractic is I've created a program and an audio series called "The 28 Laws of Chiropractic Attractability," and it's all tied to this quote. Once we understand the concept of abundance and attraction, we attract everything into our lives: people, places, and things. We attract the good, bad, and ugly. When that happens, you start to learn the secrets of this and you start to tap into this. You then

Inspire Chiropractic

create success, and then you create abundance. It is like you do not work at it. You play and you create a great life. It's not hard; you just know it's there and the momentum builds and builds until you can think something and it suddenly presents itself in your life. Success is based on tapping into this.

Do you think there is any such thing as failure in life, or are there just lessons to be learned?

Totally just lessons. Failure is a really important word to define for ourselves as individuals. Some people will say sickness or death or problems are failures, and yes, those things are there, but one of the secrets that Napoleon Hill tapped into is that you can learn from obstacles. I don't even use the word "failure"; I say "obstacles" or "challenges." Some of them are wonderful. In fact, you might be going down a path and a so-called "failure" can take you on a different path, and you might look back and say, "Oh my God, I couldn't have gotten to where I am now if that had not occurred in my life."

Can you share some of these obstacles you have encountered in you life and what lessons they have taught you?

Actually, that's how I got into chiropractic. I was involved in microbiology and medicine and cancer research. If I hadn't said, "My God, this is NOT what I want to be doing in my life," I wouldn't have even been open to this intuitive path of following chiropractic. This has happened to me many times. I'd wake up one day and say I loved to practice, and then I'd wake up one day and say that something wasn't right and I needed to make a change. Some people would look at it as a real failure or obstacle every time I realized, "Oh my God, I'm not doing what I am destined to do." I just used it as a springboard.

After I had sold my practice Dr. Reikman asked me to work with him at Palmer College. This required my husband selling his practice, and the two of us and our three sons all moved to Davenport, Iowa. That was an okay place, but it wasn't OUR place. If we hadn't gone through some of the challenges of not loving where we lived that year, I don't know if we would have ended up in Boulder, Colorado, and we love it here. I wake up everyday and say, "Oh my God, I love where I live".

Those are just a couple of examples. I also had a really dear

Dr. Janice Hughes

friend of mine die from breast cancer. That's an obstacle. That's a challenge. She had three sons like I do, and there are many other parallels between her life and mine. Although her death has been very hard, she gave be a real gift by showing me that we don't know if there will be a tomorrow.

Challenges are all around us. Are they failures, or are they obstacles? I have decided that they are opportunities.

Napoleon Hill talks about the importance of a mastermind group. If you could put together your ultimate mastermind group, using people both living and dead, who would you have in your group?

I love the definition of a mastermind. Anyone I can learn from is included in my board of directors. That includes people like Oprah Winfrey. John DeMartini was a real mentor and influence in my life. I'd also include Mother Theresa. She isn't physically here anymore, but she had various qualities and characteristics that are really pertinent to me. I use Churchill on my board of directors. I have Lance Armstrong. I have my nephew, Tate, even though he's only four years old. I have one of my previous patients who passed away – a young girl named Tara. She was in a bad car accident, so they took her to the hospital and gave her some medicines that caused her to pass away. That happened really early in my career and I took it very personally. I obviously hadn't taught her enough for her to advocate on her own behalf, since she had a right not to have those medications.

You can see I have a blend of people in my mastermind group. I also try to focus on people that are living so I can watch and learn from them, like Mark Victor Hansen and Tony Robbins.

In *Think and Grow Rich*, Napoleon Hill talks about 13 steps to riches: desire, faith, auto suggestion, specialized knowledge, imagination, organized planning, decision, persistence, power of the master mind, the mystery of sex transmutation , the sub-conscience mind, the brain, and the sixth sense. Which are a few of your favorites and why?

My number one favorite is decision. I believe that the number one key to success is decisiveness. Decision is very pertinent in the way I coach and the way I lead my life. Instead of waiting to be one hundred percent certain, Jack Welch taught me that even by the time you're about seventy percent leaning one way, you

Inspire Chiropractic

can harness that and make the decision. If you don't do that in the business world, somebody else will come to market with the product or with the idea. Decisiveness leads to a lot of great things!

My second favorite on that list is the sixth sense. It has a lot to do with intuition. Many people meditate to tap into intuition, or use the thought flashes that BJ described. That quiet time is such an important part of our lives. Wisdom is understanding this and learning to bring some of that quiet time into your life.

The third thing on that list that has become really pertinent to me in the last couple years is faith. Faith is believing that there is something bigger than us, that there are principles to follow and not just the demands of our left-brain. Many people read Napoleon Hill. Like I said before, as a teenager, a copy of it was given to me, and I wasn't comfortable with it at that point. I was arrogant and egotistical, so I didn't read it. I didn't have enough faith in the author or even in the person that handed me the book. In the last few years, faith has become a strong driving force for me.

He says at the end of the book that before any of these steps can be put into practice, we have to clear three enemies out of our lives: indecision, doubt, and fear. Can you share with us tools that you have used to clear these enemies out of your life?

All of us have different personalities. Some personalities are more fear-driven or more fear-based, but all personalities experience some level of fear in their lives. We hear that fear is false evidence that appears real. Fear leads to indecision. Others aren't good at making decisions, which leads to doubt and fear. They are all tied together.

A tool I use in my own life and in my coaching is to let fear be my guide. It knows what I am afraid of, and it knows if there is any truth to the fiction that frightens me. I pay attention to that and I write it down. Instead of letting it immobilize me, I ask, "How can I take one step into this?" "What is the next simplest step I can take?"

There are a lot of tools that people can use to address these three things.

Dr. Janice Hughes

Can you share with us some of you favorite books or authors and some of the reasons you think they are beneficial?

That's a wonderful question. I could go on for days about books.

From the financial realm, I recommend *The Richest Man In Babylon*. It's a very basic book. It teaches good principles: pay your self-first, the ten percent rule. There's a Canadian author named David Chilton who wrote a book called *The Wealthy Barber*, which is a lot like the *The Richest Man In Babylon*. They both have very tangible principles, and I think everybody should have one or both of those books and should come back to them at least once a year.

Obviously, *Think and Grow Rich* is on my list. There are many books based on the Napoleon Hill Foundation, and a lot of their resources are wonderful. I also really like the Robert Kiosaki books, *The Rich Dad/Poor Dad series*.

People shouldn't just have books; I also highly recommend CDs. Larry Markson has a phenomenal product called *The Prosperity Faucet*.

People should read from multiple categories of books. I love Wayne Dyer – he wrote *The Manifestation Principle*. I love Chopra. Every personality is going to be different: I suggest that people who are more analytical get books with more data and information and detail. You might go more for some of the good financial planners and knowledge books. Everyone's different, but the books I suggested are a wonderful foundation for anyone to start with.

Do you have any parting words of advice for us?

My favorite quote is by Buddha. It says, "How you live one day is how you live your life." Napoleon Hill based many of his universal principles on this idea. Instead of thinking, "I'll get to this someday, I'll do that when I have enough money, or I'll do that when I'm more successful," I suggest looking at that quote and asking yourself, "What kind of things am I doing now?" Are you doing things today that will lead you to where you want to go? Are you reading these principles, studying these principles, and being coached? Being coached is such a critical piece in all of this.

Inspire Chiropractic

You may reach Dr. Janice Hughes at:
www.drjanicehughes.com
www.2inspireonline.com

Chapter 6

DR. DENNIS PERMAN
Co-founder of *The Masters Circle*

"The concept of thinking a certain way, the concept of setting your inner mechanisms for success was very radical for me."
-Dr. Dennis Perman

𝒟r. Dennis Perman DC, healer, author, speaker, producer and coach, is co-founder of *The Masters Circle*, a leadership coaching and practice building company for chiropractors. His original concepts on identity, self development, Capacity Technology™ and practice fulfillment have inspired thousands of healers and demonstrated practical applications of universal laws that influence millions of chiropractic patients. The author of "The Column," "The Masters Guide" and many CD albums, and the executive producer of TMCtv, the world's largest online video library for chiropractors, he continues to blaze new trails in chiropractic education, personal growth and success.

> "So, by showing up with healing consciousness, not just as a skillful mechanic, but with a genuine understanding of the way that the universe works, above-down, inside-out, I think that this distinction is one that I'm incredibly proud of."
> – Dr. Dennis Perman

Inspire Chiropractic

Notes from the editors:

Many years ago, while a student, I walked into the library at Palmer College of Chiropractic and discovered a 30-day journey that proved to be my first experience with personal development. It was the most life-changing experience I have ever had. I had found *Personal Power*, a 30-day program by Anthony Robbins.

Later, when I first met Dr. Dennis Perman, he was as tall as Anthony Robbins. In fact, before I had the pleasure of hearing him speak, I was already comparing his height to Tony's. When Dr. Perman approached the stage, I experienced a giant present with a very calm and gentle manner. This was much different to the way Anthony Robbins presents: in your face, jumping up and down. Dr. Perman's presentation resembled that of an artist and I took in every word he spoke.

It is now my pleasure to introduce Dr. Perman. In this exclusive interview, you will learn how Napoleon Hill's philosophy helped shape a healthy attitude toward money in the subconscious mind of this great legend in chiropractic. You will get to experience firsthand how the principles of Hill's concepts of mastermind, auto-suggestion, decision, burning desire, and the power of faith boosted a doctor with a not so successful practice to become mega-successful in his own practice and a consultant to other doctors. Dr. Perman will also share with you some of the personal tools he uses to help him experience richness of life, or what he calls fulfillment. You will learn what the six P's mean and how they will help you into developing your riches. Most importantly, Dr. Perman shares how Napoleon Hill's *Think and Grow Rich* helped him cultivate a money consciousness as opposed to that of a skillful mechanic.

-Dr. Matt Hammett

Dr. Trish Hammett interviewing Dr. Dennis Perman:

To start out, you're very, very well known in chiropractic. For the one or two people out there who aren't familiar with you and your role in chiropractic, can you tell us about your

Dr. Dennis Perman

background in chiropractic?

Sure. I didn't know anything about chiropractic growing up. I was in grad school at Johns Hopkins University and my father called me up and said, "I am going to go to chiropractic college." I said, "what's that?" He said, "well, it's kind of a natural doctor." I said, "really?" So my dad started school and he told me shortly thereafter that he was enjoying it but he thought it was a perfect fit for me. So it was my dad, Dr. William Perman, that got me involved in chiropractic in the first place. I went to New York Chiropractic College, graduated in 1978. Shortly thereafter, I was doing okay in practice. I was seeing about 100 people a week and making about $100 a week. I realized that there must be more to it. I became aware of a gentleman named Larry Markson, Dr. Markson, who became my coach and mentor.

I joined Markson Management and was a successful member between 1980 and 1987. Then I decided I wanted to go into show business full time because I wanted there to be some kind of a media spokesperson for chiropractic. There wasn't one at the time. On the way to doing that, Larry said, "well, why don't you just come to work for me and I'll put you on stage?" So I became a consultant. I worked for Markson Management Services for five years, between '87 and '92.

Then I went out to develop my own consulting company that was called Consultant On Call. It was the first identity-based company -- in other words, the first company that acknowledged very clearly that "who you are determines how well what you do works," that "success comes from you, not to you." Most companies at the time were strategy based and that's the reason why I decided to create a new entity that was based more on the being than the doing.

Well, I did very well and four years later Dr. Markson approached me and said, "I like what you're doing. Why don't we merge our companies?" So I became partners with Larry in 1996. What was then known as Markson Management went away and the new entity was called *The Masters*. For three years, Larry and I ran *The Masters*. Then we decided we wanted to branch out more. We welcomed Dr. Bob Hoffman into our partnership and the new entity became known as *The Masters Circle*. We've gone forward from 2000 to now. It's now coming up on 2009. Larry is now retired from *The Masters Circle*, but Bob and I continue to run *TMC*.

In regards to Napoleon Hill's *Think & Grow Rich*, when was the first time you were introduced to this book?

The first time I was introduced to *Think & Grow Rich* was through Larry. It was 1981 and Larry mentioned it from the stage and I got an instant feeling that this was something I needed to know more about. The concept of the mastermind, the concept of auto-suggestion, being decisive, these were concepts that were built into my success training right from the beginning. And when I pressed Larry on where he learned these things, he pointed me towards *Think & Grow Rich*. So I first read *Think & Grow Rich* 27 years ago.

Can you give us an overview of how this book and philosophies have impacted your life?

Absolutely. The concept of thinking a certain way, the concept of setting your inner mechanisms for success was very radical for me. It was easy for me to see how working hard could make you more successful. But I always worked hard and I only got to a certain point. It was only when I started recognizing that the inner mechanisms of success, the thought process, recognizing the role of belief, recognizing the role of having a definite sense of purpose and being decisive enough to pursue that, those were vital parts of my evolution. But probably the greatest part was the awareness of the mastermind.

The mastermind was a concept that I was very unfamiliar with because I was pretty much a Lone Ranger. I was a bright guy. I always did well in anything intellectually. I rarely sought outside help. When I became aware that I could amplify my power multifold by interfacing with other people, especially other people who had expertise outside of mine, I discovered that I could tap into those information fields in a way that added more gravity, more value, more of a profound knowledge to what it was I was doing. I felt like I was exploring wisdom for the first time. I always had knowledge, but by recognizing the power of the mastermind, I felt like I was tapping into real wisdom.

In *Think & Grow Rich*, the publisher's preface says that riches cannot always be measured in money. We'd like to hear your thoughts on this statement and your own personal definition of what it means to be rich.

Dr. Dennis Perman

Wow, great question. Yes, it is quite clear that success in and of itself is overrated. That's why in our work we concentrate more on fulfillment. Fulfillment is success plus happiness and satisfaction. Success in and of itself, a monetary success, it's only satisfying if that's the definition of riches for you. My experience is that a rich life is a life that is complete in the ways that each individual wants it to be complete. That's what fulfillment is made of.

So in my model, there are six Ps that go into the development of riches. There is your sense of Purpose. There are Personal goals. There are Professional goals. There are People goals. There are Prosperity goals. And there are Play goals. So you can play by walking on the beach. It doesn't cost any money. You can feel prosperous just by looking into your baby's eyes or your lover's eyes. You can have a richness of the kind of people you get to associate with, as I do every single day. To limit the experience of success and riches only to financial would be a terrible oversimplification. Riches or success in general are defined by each individual's perspective. And that's a big chunk of the work that I do with my coaching, is helping people to develop a perspective on what success looks like for them. For some people, money's very important and there's nothing wrong with that. But for some people, money is only part of it. And the willingness to explore through these six Ps what the entirety of fulfillment looks like for you sets the stage for real riches, not just financial riches.

> "Yes, success comes from you, not to you. Who you are determines how well what you do works."

You kind of answered my next question a little bit, but maybe there's something you'd like to expound on. Do you think that being rich and being successful is the same thing and what's the difference?

Well, it's only the same thing if the individual's definition of success is primarily financial. And there are indeed people like that and there's nothing wrong with that. But I know people who are not financially successful, but who feel extremely fulfilled by what they do. Now, the obvious examples are the Mother Teresas and the individuals who have committed their lives to service. They experience riches that go far beyond anything that could be purchased. But I really think, since I'm an identity-based guy, I really think that the definition of success and riches is a personal one. I know that I am richest when I am with my

Inspire Chiropractic

wife and my children. I wouldn't need any money... Obviously, you need money to live, but I wouldn't need any money in order to feel rich if I have that experience. Likewise with my creativity. It's a very important aspect of my life to play music, to write, to experience all different aspects of creativity, art and music and video. I love that. So to me, if I'm in a situation where I'm experiencing these things that are really important to me, I feel rich whether I have money or not.

So my suggestion to people who are wondering what it takes to be successful is to begin by defining what success is for them. The moment you do that, your strategies become much clearer, because by showing up a certain way and by being willing to take actions based on how you show up, you can pursue success on your terms. You don't have to be locked into somebody else's definition of it.

Do you happen to have a personal motto for success?

Yes, success comes from you, not to you. Who you are determines how well what you do works.

I've heard that before.

I'm glad.

In *Think & Grow Rich*, Napoleon Hill includes the following quote, "a peculiar thing about this secret of riches is that those who once acquire it and use it find themselves literally swept on to success, but with little effort and they never again submit to failure." We'd like to hear your thoughts on this statement.

This is one of the places where maybe I have some shades of difference with Hill, because I think that the concept of failure is terribly misrepresented in people's thinking. It's impossible to fail unless you quit. If you're in the game, then you're getting feedback. Some of the things you do will not work and some of them will. If you accept that it would be unreasonable to have perfect results based on perfect strategies and perfect execution every time, if you realize that's an unreasonable expectation, then you start to look at failure as feedback. You start to look at what seems like failure as new input that guides you toward greater successes. Indeed, out of some of what seemed like my worst moments, I've been able to make some of my greatest

Dr. Dennis Perman

breakthroughs.

So my read on this is not that once you dial into success, it never stops, but rather, once you become the kind of person who can create success in his or her life, you never lose that option. You can choose to perceive what's going on around you in such a way that it takes you towards success, even if it doesn't feel good and even if it wasn't the outcome you expected. Based on that, my perception is that, yes, as you become a successful person inside out, you always have access to that process. But never dread failure. Welcome and embrace it, because it's actually important information that guides you towards your next greater success.

Could you share with us some "failures" that you've encountered in your journey through life and what lessons they've taught you?

Sure. Well, when I first started practice, I was ill equipped to handle the financial end of practice. I knew very little about money. I was fortunate enough to grow up in an affluent household and I never really had to think too much about it. All of a sudden, I'm out in practice, interfacing with a world of finances that I really had very little experience with. As a result, as I started building my practice, I wasn't doing a good job either collecting or managing my money. I really didn't know about it. So I ran into some serious financial issues along the way. It was as a result of my exposure to the thinking that came from Dr. Markson and also from *Think & Grow Rich*, that I was able to establish a new relationship with money. If I hadn't had that painful problem, if I hadn't had those issues, I probably never would have been directed towards learning all these magnificent things that have made my career so enjoyable and so productive.

I'll give you one more. I had an experience not long ago, a couple of years ago, where I had a mountain bike accident where I joined the "endo" club. Endo means end over end. I flipped over the handlebars, landed hard on my shoulder and dislocated my shoulder. I had never experienced any pain like that before. I'd never been sick. I've never been in a hospital, never had any surgery. Where's some wood to knock? Here we go. I'm 55 years old and I've never had a serious health problem. I felt invulnerable. When I had this injury, it rocked my world because just like buying into the idea that Hill was talking

Inspire Chiropractic

about before, that once you're on a roll, you can expect it to continue. I expected to be healthy every day of my life. When I injured myself, I couldn't believe it. I thought that I was blessed to never get injured and in some bizarre way, I almost felt like God had forsaken me. When you're in a lot of pain, your mind does a lot of crazy things. As I healed, I realized that there was incredible opportunity here for me to take much better care of myself physically than I ever had before. I developed a different attitude toward exercise, a different attitude toward nutrition, a different attitude towards my chiropractic adjustments. And, as such, I was able to use that injury, that "failure," which was very embarrassing, being with people and being the guy who ends up on the ground looking up, with everybody going, "oh, look, his shoulder's hanging out." That was a very humiliating position for me. Yet, out of that experience grew a real appreciation for things that I had already had a pretty good relationship with, but I was able to deepen my relationship with my sense of self, knowing that through those "imperfections" I was able to make myself more perfect.

You already touched on how important the concept of mastermind has been to you.

Yes.

If you could put together your ultimate mastermind group, from people both living and dead, who would you have in your group?

Well, that's going to be kind of easy for me, because I already do a process that I call mental mastermind that I have a very intimate relationship with numerous people, both living and dead. Let me share a couple of them with you. Anthony

"Taking one of the great books of all time, *Think & Grow Rich*, and adding your spin to it. I couldn't applaud this project any more, because I believe that by doing so, not only do you pay honor to Napoleon Hill, but you also do what he would have hoped you would do. By using the very same principles that he teaches, you are applying them in the context of creating a brand new vision and a brand new work that's going to have a very significant impact on the people who come in contact with it."

Dr. Dennis Perman

Robbins is in my mastermind because of his personal power. B. J. Palmer is in my mastermind because of his incredible vision and commitment. I'm going around the table. Mother Teresa is in my mastermind because of her incredible love. My lovely wife, Regina, is in my mastermind because of her incredible sense of dedication to the most important things in life. I use these mastermind interchanges to help me solve problems, but more important to help me create a grander vision. Guy Riekeman sits at my table. Larry Markson sits at my table. Bob Hoffman sits at my table.

I feel very blessed to have met some of the most amazing people in the world throughout my journey. What I've discovered is that as I encounter new people and get to know them, I can add them into my mastermind. Michael Gerber is part of my mastermind because of his incredible business expertise. Deepak Chopra is part of my mastermind because of his amazing benevolence in integrating the medical world with the natural healing world.

I change people in and out at times because I recognize that I may need a different mastermind team, depending on what's going on. Right now, with some business challenges, I've got Gerber sitting front and center, helping me understand the things I need to do in order to manufacture the right kind of changes I need. But I've had Abraham Lincoln sitting at my mastermind. I've had George Washington sitting at my mastermind. I've had Buddha and Jesus Christ sitting at my mastermind. I feel very blessed in having been exposed to so many wonderful people and I think that the more people embrace the concept of masterminding, both physical masterminding with people and also mental masterminding, internal masterminding, I believe that this is one of the ways that we're going to create the most power and the most good that we possibly can.

Great, thank you. In the book, *Think & Grow Rich*, Napoleon Hill lists out thirteen steps to riches. He talks about desire, faith, auto-suggestion, specialized knowledge, imagination, organized planning, decision, persistence, power of the mastermind, mystery of sex transmutation, the subconscious mind, the brain, and the sixth sense. Of these steps, which are a few of your favorite principles and why?

Well, I already talked about the mastermind, so I won't spend too

Inspire Chiropractic

much time on that. For me, imagination is huge. I like to think of myself as a creative person, as I mentioned before. I feel like my imagination is one of my strongest suits, so I pay special attention to doing imagination and visualization processes numerous times each day. I feel like it creates the backdrop for me to be able to take massive action.

Auto-suggestion is also very big for me because I feel very strongly about affirmation and visualization working together as important tools toward goal setting.

But if I had to pick one that I felt I couldn't do without and one that I was not naturally gifted at, one that I had to develop in myself, it would have to be decision. Decisiveness is the difference that makes the difference in great achievers. If somebody is unwilling to decide, then they cannot fully commit and if they cannot fully commit, then they cannot resolve and make the changes that need to be made. So I feel like if someone is willing to be decisive, if they're willing to bring themselves to a definite decision, then that is the trigger that launches all the success process.

Then he goes on to say, there at the end of the book, that before any of these steps can be put into practice, we have to clear three enemies out of our mind—indecision, doubt, and fear. Can you share with us tools that you used to clear those enemies out of your way?

Absolutely, absolutely. You know, with my work with Anthony Robbins, I had the privilege of being a master trainer for him for over a decade, meaning I got to train his instructors. So I'm very, very familiar with his work. My concept on this may be a little different from many. I don't think that indecision, doubt, and fear are something. I think they're the lack of something. I think they're the absence of something. If you're in a room with no windows and there's a light switch in there and it's flipped up, then we would say the light is on. If you flip the light switch down, we would say, now it's dark in here. Well, the question is, is the darkness something that shows up when the light goes away or is it actually a nothing that gets filled in when the light goes on? My contention is that, like darkness, indecision, doubt, and fear are the absence of something.

So the way to deal with them is to build the resources that are the opposite of them—decisiveness, certainty, positive

Dr. Dennis Perman

expectancy—and as you build those resources, you'll find that, just like when you put the light switch on, the darkness seems to go away, but it doesn't, because it was never there in the first place. Indecision, doubt, and fear are not there. We perceive them to be there. And as soon as you build resources to fill in the place where those things weren't, you never have to worry about them again.

What a fantastic perspective. We have some more time left, so why don't we move to a few personal questions? Can you share with us what you consider to be some of the highlights and accomplishments of both your personal and professional life?

Sure. The thing that I am proudest of in my life is my marriage. I am incredibly blessed. My lovely wife, Regina, is my best friend. She's the smartest person I know and I enjoy every second I'm

> "Understanding things natural -- understanding that things happen as they should, that we live in a cause and effect universe -- understanding that there is a divine, above-down, inside-out perspective that you can develop from watching what happens in the healing process."

with her and I miss her every second I'm not with her. We met when we were 17. I'm now 55, so we've been together 38 years, 30 years of marriage. The thing I'm proudest of is that she wants me, because a beautiful, intelligent, incredibly talented woman like this could have anybody that she wanted. And the fact that she picked me is my greatest blessing in life. Likewise, my children, who fortunately are much more like her than like me. They are intelligent. They are kind. They understand love. They're spiritual. They're willing to do what it takes in order to create successes in their own lives. And I'm amazingly proud of that.

Professionally, I think the thing I'm probably proudest of is the evidence of my creativity. I write a column every week that goes out to thousands of chiropractic offices that I get wonderful feedback on, *The Message of the Week*. I've recently published a compilation, an anthology over the last decade. I don't think there are too many online columnists who have been writing for

Inspire Chiropractic

ten solid years without a stop. So I was very proud of my work and I compiled it into a book called *The Column* that is a very interesting retrospective over the last ten years. It's kind of like the literary equivalent of time-lapse photography. I write these on Sunday and they're published every Monday morning, so there's a lot of really interesting stuff in there. 9/11 is in there, and the Yankees' great season in '98 is in there. Numerous personal milestones are in there as well.

Professionally, I'm proud of being a chiropractor. I'm proud that I was guided in this direction because I feel that chiropractic gave me a panoramic view on philosophies that, prior to my time as a chiropractor, I really only viewed peripherally. Understanding things natural -- understanding that things happen as they should, that we live in a cause and effect universe -- understanding that there is a divine, above-down, inside-out perspective that you can develop from watching what happens in the healing process. I feel incredibly blessed for having had the opportunity to be a healer and over the last 20 years to train healers, so that they can learn not just chiropractic technique and not just healing technique, but they could learn that it's who you are that determines how well what you do works. So, by showing up with healing consciousness, not just as a skillful mechanic, but with a genuine understanding of the way that the universe works, above-down, inside-out, I think that this distinction is one that I'm incredibly proud of.

I'm also proud of the fact that I've been able to maintain a variety of different interests. I love music. I've been playing music since I was five years old. I play guitar and piano. I write songs. I love to do song parodies. I'm very, very proud of this outlet for my creativity because I feel that an artist is tapping into energies that are some of the most divine, the most transcendent energies there are. I really enjoy taking somebody else's work and working on it some more, so that I can make it my own and that is exactly what you're doing. Taking one of the great books of all time, *Think & Grow Rich*, and adding your spin to it. I couldn't applaud this project any more, because I believe that by doing so, not only do you pay honor to Napoleon Hill, but you also do what he would have hoped you would do. By using the very same principles that he teaches, you are applying them in the context of creating a brand new vision and a brand new work that's going to have a very significant impact on the people who come in contact with it.

Dr. Dennis Perman

Do you have any regrets in life?

No.

Can you share some of your favorite books and authors and explain why you think these books and authors are worthy of us getting to know them?

Sure. I enjoy Anthony Robbins, *Unlimited Power, Awaken the Giant Within,* magnificent books. I am a big fan of Neale Donald Walsch; the entire *Conversations With God* series is very profound. I like Wayne Dyer, *Real Magic, Sacred Self, Manifest Your Destiny.* I think those books are very profound. I enjoy Deepak Copra, take your pick; they're all pretty good. His most recent novel, *Why Is God Laughing?,* I think is pretty terrific, and also *The Seven Spiritual Laws of Success.* What else? Don Miguel Ruiz, *The Four Agreements.* I know I'm going to leave books out. When you send it to me to edit, I'll make sure the list is complete.

I'm an avid reader. *Think & Grow Rich* has to be in there, of course. But there are so many. I read between 30 and 50 books a year. *The Dynamic Laws of Prosperity* by Catherine Ponder. *E-Myth Mastery* by Michael Gerber. *The Wisdom of the Enneagram* by Don Richard Riso and Russ Hudson. *Everyday Enlightenment* by Dan Millman. *The Seven Habits of Highly Effective People* by Steven Covey. *Discover Your Destiny* by Robin Sharma. *Power vs. Force* by David Hawkins. *Failing Forward* by John Maxwell. *Discover Wellness* by Bob Hoffman and Jason Deitch. The poetry of Rumi or Dogen. *The Six Pillars of Self Esteem* by Nathaniel Branden. *Getting Things Done* by David Allen. *How To Think Like Leonardo Da Vinci* by Michael Gelb. There are so many great ones, no way to list them all. I publish a book list every year of my favorite reading. If you like, I'll go through it and make sure I haven't left anything important out.

Do you have any parting words of advice for us?

Yes. Yes, I do. Life is an inside-out game. The more we recognize that what we bring to it is going to be the major component of what we get out of it, the more likely we stop spinning our wheels and worrying about what somebody else is going to think or do. There's only two kinds of things in the world, things you can do something about and things you can't

Inspire Chiropractic

do nothing about. The more you learn to stay focused on the things you can do something about, the more likely it is that you develop yourself into the kind of you that would make the life that you really want.

One more thought. You can only grow as great as your weaker areas permit. What that means is that most people are so hung up on their strengths, on playing their strengths, that they forget that improvement is about being willing to look at the stuff you're not quite so good at yet. The laws of capacity technology, another thing I should mention that I'm very proud of, that I've worked on developing over the last 20 years, is a study of behavior and action that helps you understand how to invest yourself so that you get the best results possible. What it basically says is you can't get nine ounces into an eight-ounce glass. Even though that sounds like a goofy statement, what it really means is if you expect to accomplish at a great level, you must grow yourself into the kind of person who could. It's a be-do-have universe. The more that you learn how to be the kind of person that you can be at your best, the more likely that what you do brings you to the opportunity so you can have what you want to have.

Thank you.

You may reach Dr. Dennis Perman at:

The Masters Circle, Inc.
100 Jericho Quadrangle, Suite 140
Jericho, New York 11753
1-800-451-4514
bob@themasterscircle.com
www.themasterscircle.com

Dr. Dennis Perman

NOTES:

Chapter 7

DR. JOAN FALLON
CEO and Founder of Curemark

"People think of energy as flowing in one direction – towards richness, towards success – but sometimes the energy flows the opposite way."
-Dr. Joan Fallon

Dr. Fallon is presently the CEO of Curemark. After 26 years of clinical practice in the area of chiropractic pediatrics, and pediatric development, Dr. Fallon founded Curemark a biotechnology company with visionary science based on sound clinical observations made during her tenure as a clinician.

> "Opportunity is one of the most important things that can bring richness and success. I try to cultivate the idea of opportunity for children that I treat. I want them to know that they are never locked into being something or doing something, but that they have a choice."
> -Dr. Joan Fallon

Having filed her first patent application in 1999, Dr. Fallon has worked to research autism and related disorders as well as to bring her findings to a platform for commercialization. She has both clinical

Dr. Joan Fallon

experience as well as academic experience having served as an assistant professor of Natural Sciences and Mathematics at Yeshiva University. Dr. Fallon has also been an integral part of two very successful ventures, which were both unprecedented at the time of formation. Dr. Fallon was a board member at Oxford Health Plans, and was instrumental in achieving underwriting authority for alternative and complementary medicine from New York State when none had ever existed. She also was able to implement a health plan for Oxford involving children that was cost effective and increased their level of healthcare tremendously.

Dr. Fallon's discovery of the biomarker for autism and AD/HD and her vast array of the intellectual property in the area of gastrointestinal secretory deficiencies, forms the basis of Curemark. Dr. Fallon has written numerous scholarly articles, and has lectured around the world on developmental problems in the pediatric population. She has served on the Board of directors of the ICA and Kentuckiana Children's Center. Dr. Fallon was one of the first physicians of any type to enter Romania and to help determine the state of the Romanian orphanages as an emissary of the US government. She presently serves as an advisor to the NY Yankees for disability services for the new Yankee Stadium. She is a Fellow of the International College of Chiropractic Pediatrics, she has a BA degree from Franklin and Marshall College, a DC degree from Palmer College of Chiropractic, and has completed her work for the MSc in clinical investigation from Harvard University's joint program with Massachusetts General Hospital. She resides in Bronxville, NY.

Notes from the editors:

Recently, there was a press release from PRnewswire that read as follows:

> Curemark Receives Investigational New Drug Clearance for CM-AT for Autism
>
> "Curemark, LLC, a drug research and development company focused on the treatment of neurological

Inspire Chiropractic

diseases, announced today that the U.S. Food and Drug Administration (FDA) has cleared the company's investigational new drug (IND) application to initiate its pivotal Phase III clinical trial of CM-AT for the treatment of autism.

As part of this IND, the FDA has agreed that Curemark may proceed directly into pivotal Phase III clinical trials in patients with autism. The FDA has reviewed the quality, safety and efficacy data generated by Curemark in pediatric patients with autism. In addition, the FDA has provided written guidance on the trial protocol. The company expects to begin Phase III clinical trials at multiple sites across the U.S. in the second quarter of 2009.

"FDA clearance of the CM-AT IND for the pivotal Phase III trial is an important milestone for Curemark," commented Dr. Joan Fallon, Curemark's CEO. "With 1 in 150 children diagnosed with autism, we have children who are suffering. We are very excited about the opportunity to enter a Phase III trial for this ever-growing population of children.'"

In this exclusive interview with the legendary Dr. Joan Fallon, you will discover how she applied the philosophies of Napoleon Hill to achieve this great success. You will learn that she believes there is no failure, just a change in direction; and, this change in direction sets up a new course in life. Today, Dr. Fallon is poised at the doorstep of an innovative treatment for autism, because she knew how to "change course."

-Dr. Matt Hammett

Dr. Trish Hammett interviewing Dr. Joan Fallon:

How were you first introduced to Napoleon Hill's *Think & Grow Rich*?

I have been aware of the work for a very long time and I have read it throughout my life at various times when I have needed to.

How has its philosophies impacted your life?

Dr. Joan Fallon

I think that richness is really richness of spirit. My parents were instrumental in looking at richness of spirit as a quality of life. I have grown up with that philosophy, and Hill's book just reinforced it for me in print.

In the publisher's preface, there is a quote that says "riches cannot always be measured in money." We would like to hear your thoughts on that statement and also what your personal definition of being rich is.

It is absolutely true. Riches cannot be measured in money. That is something that was instilled in my brother and me. Our parents always encouraged us to do what made us happy. They tried to create a richness of spirit in terms of opportunities for us, and they gave us a lot of richness in our experiences as we were growing up. That was very important to me. If you have richness of spirit, success just follows.

Tell us a little bit more about your background in chiropractic.

I graduated in 1983 from Palmer, and I had the distinct pleasure of having Dr. Maxine McMullen as one of my mentors. Dr. McMullen is very involved with pediatrics. I worked in her clinic with her while I was going to school, so I was able to see a lot of children even before I graduated. When I got out of chiropractic school, I naturally attracted a lot of children and a lot of pregnant women, so my practice has basically been children for the past 25 years. That has been wonderful for me.

You mentioned richness of spirit and how success naturally follows it. Do you think that being rich and being successful is the same thing?

"Things are never the same once you are swept up by your richness of spirit."

There are probably some who are very rich of spirit who are not necessarily what other people would call successful. If success were measured by money, then some people who are rich in spirit would be considered unsuccessful. However, if success is the ability to be proud of what you have done, then richness of spirit and success are one in the same.

Do you have a person motto for success?

Inspire Chiropractic

Opportunity is one of the most important things that can bring richness and success. I try to cultivate the idea of opportunity for children that I treat. I want them to know that they are never locked into being something or doing something, but that they have a choice. Choice is what chiropractic is all about. We give people a choice of healthcare. I have tried to teach children that they have choices in life. From that, everything else follows.

Another quote from the book says that those who acquire this secret of riches find themselves literally swept on to success, but with little effort, and they never again submit to failure. We would like to hear your thoughts on that statement.

If you follow your richness of spirit, it is like a tsunami. A tsunami is something that swells up behind and just washes over the shore. While people think of that as a destructive force, that kind of washing can also be very constructive. Things are never the same once you are swept up by your richness of spirit. The landscape changes forever. Everything comes behind it, and as a result, it just keeps coming.

Is there any such thing as failure in life, or are they simply lessons to be learned?

I look at failures as opportunities. Life is about energy. People think of energy as flowing in one direction – towards richness, towards success – but sometimes the energy flows the opposite way. Yet it still gets you where you need to go. I never look at it as a failure. I just look at it as a change in the direction of my energy. Sometimes that change can alter all the rest of the energies that are going forward and that alteration can bring you to the success you are looking for. I do not believe in failure; I believe in changing course.

Can you give us any examples of these changes in direction, or opportunities to learn, that you have encountered? What lessons did they teach you?

I am involved in a change of energy even right now. It is not failure, just a change in energy. As a result of working with children for 25 years, many in which have been disabled, I have had the opportunity to work with a lot of children who have autism. The autism epidemic came up in the 90's and I was able

Dr. Joan Fallon

to be part of it. I saw a lot of children and worked hard to figure out what was going on.

Through the course of working with these children with autism, I noticed they have unique diets and unique ways of eating. This had already been observed by scientists, but I figured out through a test that these children do not digest protein. As a result of not digesting protein, they were not getting the amino acids that they needed.

I had a brother who was an inventor, and he said I should patent that discovery. The next thing I knew, I had a patent and I had a different mission. I had a different place to put my energies: towards giving children therapy to help their autism.

Two years ago, I changed course again. An opportunity presented itself and I was able to form a corporation that is working on enzyme replacements for children with autism. That was a change in opportunity for me. I hope that it will help not just in one-on-one doctor and patient relationships, but countless numbers of children.

Napoleon Hill talked about the importance of a mastermind group. If you could put together your ultimate mastermind group from people both living and dead, who would be in your group?

I have always had my own little board of directors, people I can bounce things off of. The first person I would have in that group is

"If you do not have that burning desire inside of you, then motivation is not there and things do not move. The

my mother. She is a very wise woman. Her advice has never led me astray. After that, I would probably put Madeline Albright in that group. She has achieved a lot and has been a world leader in terms of changing people's perceptions of life.

There are lots of people; actually, who I think would be wonderful in a mastermind group.

Whoever I put in my group, they would need to think outside the box. That is especially important today, now that the normal infrastructure has changed, particularly in this country. How

Inspire Chiropractic

people work today is different from how they worked yesterday. Not only would my mastermind group be full of people who think outside the box, but they would know where the box is. I would put Bill Gates on my group because he has been in that space.

I would have to think some more about some other people. Nevertheless, they would have to think outside the box.

Share with us some of your favorite books and authors and who you would recommend.

"It is about opportunity. It is about not being fearful. It is about seizing what you have a burning desire to do and knowing that you can do it no matter what. It does not matter where you went to school. It does not matter what your background is. It does not matter how you grew up. We each have the opportunity to do what we have a burning desire to do."

I am not a fiction reader. I have always been a non-fiction reader, even as a child. My favorite books are Patricia Cornwell novels because of the way they approach medical things. Otherwise, I am a big biography reader. I like Goodwin and other people who write biographies.

In *Think & Grow Rich*, **Napoleon Hill has thirteen steps to riches. He looks at the following steps: desire, faith, autosuggestion, specialized knowledge, imagination, organized planning, decision,** persistence, power of the mastermind, the mystery of sex trans-mutation, the subconscious mind, the brain, and the sixth sense. **Of these steps, what are your favorite principles and why?**

Desire is the first one. If you do not have that burning desire inside of you, then motivation is not there and things do not move. The energies do not move. In addition, imagination is very important – thinking outside the box, looking at things in different ways. Without imagination, you cannot achieve what it is you have a desire to do. Persistence is enormously important, because if you have a desire and you also have imagination but you do not have persistence, you will still never accomplish what you set out to do.

Hill says that before you can put any of these steps into practice, you have to clear three enemies out of your mind. He names those as being indecision, doubt, and fear. Can you share with us some tools that you have used to clear those enemies out of your way?

The one thing I learned in practice is that I always have to trust myself and my gut instinct. It is something that I feel strongly about and I always follow. For instance, whenever I need to make a decision, I check to make sure fear is not motivating my good instincts. I am always careful to make sure that what is coming from my gut instinct is clean and real.

Fear is paralyzing. When people are fearful, they move away from what they have or what they understand. A lot of this whole financial crisis is based on fear. People are afraid to change what they have been doing with their money, and they have blind faith in corporations. A fear-based model of persona does not allow for change, for growth, or for creation.

Tell us what you like most about your work and what you feel are the rewards of your efforts.

I feel I have a wonderful, wonderful practice. Twenty-five years of taking care of children, watching them grow, watching them choose chiropractic for themselves, now and as they grow up... I have taken care of multiple generations in families, and that is so rewarding to me. I cannot think of anything that is more rewarding to me than my practice.

I had three goals in life when I was younger: I wanted to be a doctor for children, I wanted to write a book, and I wanted to teach at a university. By the time I was 30, I had basically done all three of those things. I was teaching at a university, I had written a book on chiropractic care during pregnancy, and I was seeing children in my office.

I had to redefine my goals in order to move forward with my life. As I did, I came upon my discovery with autistic children. Even though I am terribly sad that I do not get to see patients on a regular basis now, I am working toward my goal of helping children with autism.

Inspire Chiropractic

I have had multiple things in my life that have been very rewarding, from a career point of view. Seeing children, teaching them about healthcare, teaching them to take care of themselves, and helping them make choices in their lives are very important to me. Then I made a choice to help millions of children with autism.

Do you have any parting words of advice for us?

It is about opportunity. It is about not being fearful. It is about seizing what you have a burning desire to do and knowing that you can do it no matter what. It does not matter where you went to school. It does not matter what your background is. It does not matter how you grew up. We each have the opportunity to do what we have a burning desire to do.

Thank you so much.

You may reach Dr. Joan Fallon by visiting:
www.curemark.com

NOTES:

Chapter 8

DR. LARRY MARKSON
The Markson Connection
&
The Cabin Experience

"It was then I discovered that it is who you the doctors were and not what action steps they took that created their success, mediocrity or failure."
-Dr. Larry Markson

Dr. Larry Markson, Personal Empowerment, Practice Success and Prosperity Coach to over 25,000 professional offices for the past 28 years, has devoted his professional life to helping doctors and their key assistants to transform their thoughts, actions and feelings until they are able to experience the fulfillment of their life's goals.

He believes that your business, practice and/or your personal life are waiting for a leader (YOU)

> "I had the honor and pleasure to pick him (Napoleon Hill) up at the airport, carry his luggage and deliver him to the seminar hotel. What an amazing man and I had the privilege of getting to know him and pick his brain for the time it took to get him to the hotel and a few days later, back to the airport. He was quite a man and became one of my all time heroes."
> – Dr. Larry Markson

Dr. Larry Markson

to show up and that, "Who you are 'inside-the-skin' determines how well what you do works."

Now, in his fifth decade of sharing the secrets of success with audiences worldwide, he has learned that it is "successful people" who build successful businesses and lives - and that "Success comes FROM you, not TO you.

Notes from the editors:

Visualize attending class with Dr. B.J. Palmer, the original developer of chiropractic. Imagine what your conversation would be if you had the chance to sit down and talk with this renowned innovator. Napoleon Hill had that chance with Dr. Palmer. In fact, he spent private time with him in his mansion at Davenport, Iowa. Since most of us will never have that chance, I wonder what they discussed.

In this exclusive interview, we will have the chance to hear from a legend of chiropractic who also conversed with Dr. Palmer. Dr. Larry Markson had that chance. He was a student of both Dr. B.J. Palmer and Napoleon Hill; and, today, he is one of the most successful chiropractors in the history of the profession. Dr. Markson shares with us some of the insights he learned from these two masters that enabled him to go from rags to riches!

-Dr. Matt Hammett

Dr. Trish Hammett interviewing Dr. Larry Markson:

How were you first introduced to *Think & Grow Rich*?

I was first introduced to *Think & Grow Rich* when I was a student enrolled at the Palmer College of Chiropractic in Davenport, Iowa – and that was 50 years ago! The book itself was given to me as a gift by a fellow student – and it turns out that it was a pivotal moment in my life.

I distinctly remember the reaction I had after I read it. Skeptic that I was, I wondered if any of what Napoleon Hill wrote about was really true. My thinking was that it was just a book and I

Inspire Chiropractic

couldn't have been more wrong. Remember please, I was only 20 years of age at the time and this was my very first exposure to what I call, "The Positive World of Successful Thinking."

Sadly, the book made me feel better and more optimistic, but a few months I was back where I started, thinking my habitual thoughts and not actually working on the principles contain a

> "I started to work on some of the principles in the book, and my life began to change for the better. I even started a small mastermind group, where we got together for the sole purpose of discussing the contents and meanings of each chapter."

Think & Grow Rich. I guess many of us do that. We read a book and get turned on. Then with time, we ignore what we learned and stop taking the suggested action steps, and back to the beginning we go.

Seven years later, when I was failing in practice, seeing only between 30 and 70 patients a week, I picked it up again. This time I not only dedicated myself to reading it carefully, but I read it differently. I actually highlighted it, underlined it, made notes in the margin and studied the contents – and that turned me on again.

I started to work on some of the principles in the book, and my life began to change for the better. I even started a small mastermind group, where we got together for the sole purpose of discussing the contents and meanings of each chapter. A year-and-a-half later, I found myself reading more self-help books, going to seminars, doing affirmations, writing goals, visualizing the future and hanging out with others of like mind. The result was that my practice volume literally exploded and I ended up with 750 patient visits a week, with two associate doctors and I was, for the first time in my life, earning a substantial and appreciable income. How is that for a "rags to riches" story?

Obviously, you're very well-known within the chiropractic profession. For the one or two people out there who are not familiar with you, can you tell us about your background in chiropractic?

Dr. Larry Markson

I graduated in '61 as part of the B.J. Palmer Memorial Class which means that I was actually blessed enough to have had B.J. himself as one of my teachers. How cool is that? Obviously, that experience played a major role in all the success that I was going to achieve.

Anyhow, I was quite content and happy practicing chiropractic and being a featured speaker at the Parker Seminars where I was learning the platform skills that I would need in my future endeavors. All was right with the world until September 11, 1981 (20 years to a date that will live in infamy), at which time I sustained a career ending elbow injury.

> "It was then I discovered that it is who *you* the doctors were and not what actions steps they took that created

While I was under-going the obligatory nine months of rehabilitation, local colleagues started to ask me how I managed to build such a substantial practice. At first I just informally answered whatever questions they had. Then I formed a small mastermind group which met on a monthly basis and much to my surprise the doctors started to report that they were enjoying their practices more and they too were experiencing an uptick in practice volume and income.

I guess that was the catalyst that caused me to start my own practice management company, *Markson Management Services*. The success of *MMS* was greater than anything I could ever have dreamed of and at one time we had a just over one thousand clients involved in the process on learning the principles, protocols and parameters of building a more successful chiropractic practice.

> "Modeling the behavior of others is one of the major action steps I use to move me along on my journey to health, happiness and continued success."

We were teaching our member doctors the strategies of practice success – everything from how to train their

Inspire Chiropractic

Chiropractic Assistants, what hours to work, what forms to use, what software to buy, what to say to patients, how their office should be designed, how to attract more new patients and what procedures were necessary to create a service-oriented and growing chiropractic practice.

Thankfully, many of the doctors followed our systems, proven by the fact that their practices grew to new and record breaking levels of achievement. That went on for 16 years.

But, with all the success we were experiencing I knew something was not right. I began to realize although doctors were experiencing varied results even though they were in the same program. How could that be? If the procedures worked, why in the world wouldn't everyone involved be growing at the same rate and how could some not get any results at all. Of course, they rationalized that the program wasn't working for them, rather than they were not working the program.

It was then I discovered that it is who *you* the doctors were and not what action steps they took that created their success, mediocrity or failure.

> "Health, wealth, and happiness combined create the equilateral triangle and wealth is only one third of it."

It was all about the doctors self-image, confidence, self-esteem and their ability to make the right decisions, develop the skills of successful confrontation and eliminate the characteristics that causes failure – like procrastination, tardiness, sloppiness and clarity of thought and action.

So, on December 31, 1996 *Markson Management* was closed and *The Masters Circle* was born. *TMC* was vastly different from *MMS* in that it was an "identity-based" and not just a "strategy-based" company. We worked on, "who to be" as well as on "what to do," in order to create success.

I retired from *TMC* in 2006 and retired for 6 months until I just couldn't stand not being in action and working with people I loved. The first step was to write my first "head space" book entitled, "*Talking to Yourself is Not Crazy*" which I am happy to report is doing very well.

Dr. Larry Markson

Currently, *"The Cabin Experience,"* a Breaking Free – Personal Freedom Retreat for 25 individuals at a time is what is capturing my attention. Of all the businesses I have created, this is by far my favorite – mostly because of the intimate setting and that the personal breakthroughs created at *The Cabin Experience* continue to be live-changing.

I'm also on the Board of Trustees of Life University, which is something new and exciting for me.

And finally, the last act in my career is the creation of my new business (along with Dr, Brett Axelrod and Dr. Rick Markson) called *The Markson Connection*. The vision statement is self-explanatory. It says, "To gather and inspire a tribe of select chiropractors empowering them to make life-changing decisions that create lives of significance – abundant and overflowing with intention, passion, happiness and success.

In *Think & Grow Rich*, the publisher's preface states that riches cannot always be measured in money. We'd like to hear your thoughts on this statement and your own personal definition of what it means to be rich.

The publisher is definitely correct in the assessment that riches are not only a measurement of how much money one earns. I personally know many rich people who are not healthy, not happy, not fulfilled and their lives are not working. Health, wealth, and happiness combined create the equilateral triangle and wealth is only one third of it.

If you take any one of those components out of your life, it simply doesn't work. The triangle collapses. If you have riches without health, it doesn't work. If you have riches without happiness, it doesn't work. If you have health and happiness and no riches, it doesn't work. They all must work together!

People can be rich in spirit. They can be rich in their enjoyment of a wonderful family life. They can be rich with friendships that are important and impactful in their lives. They can be rich with the skill and talent of being an artist, being a musician, being a chiropractor, or helping sick people regain and maintain their health naturally. They can be rich in a lot of ways. However, while I am acutely conscious that traditionally richness is customarily defined in monetary terms, the amount of money in

Inspire Chiropractic

the bank, I believe it is much more than that.

Is being rich and being successful the same thing?

I say they are different. You can win the lottery and get rich but not be successful personally, or professionally or spiritually, etc. I read in the *New York Times* some years ago that many people who won more than one million dollars in the lottery were broke again five years later.

I think riches are a matter of the soul. Prosperity Consciousness and riches go together. Poverty is the opposite and more than just a lack of money it is a deficiency of spirit, of soul, of concept, of vision and ideas. I think being successful is what it is all about and while being rich is great it does not provide the sense of accomplishment that comes from have a great family, loving relationships, the feelings of accomplishment that comes from creating a great business or using your talents for the enjoyment and benefit of humanity.

Do you have a personal model for success?

I have tons of personal models. I'm blessed to have great personal friends who are walking, talking and living models of success, happiness and integrity. Additionally, I have had the privilege of getting to work with and know some incredible self-help gurus and over the years I have attempted to model, mirror, copy, steal and plagiarize their teaching, attitudes, actions, procedures, concepts and visions.

Additionally, I have listened to the wisdoms espoused on CD's and DVD's and the writing of the authors that speak so eloquently about self-improvement, personal growth and spiritual enlightenment.

Yes, I have models and I will continue to look for more as time goes on. Modeling the behavior of others is one of the major action steps I use to move me along on my journey to health, happiness and continued success.

In *Think & Grow Rich*, Napoleon Hill includes the following quote: "A peculiar thing about this secret of riches is that those who acquire it and use it find themselves literally swept on to success, but with little effort, and they never again submit to failure." We'd like to hear your thoughts on

Dr. Larry Markson

this statement.

I don't totally agree with that specific quote but I understand what Napoleon Hill was attempting to say.

By the way, I was fortunate enough to have lunch with Napoleon Hill himself when was a speaker at a Parker Seminar many years ago. I had the honor and pleasure to pick him up at the airport, carry his luggage and deliver him to the seminar hotel. What an amazing man and I had the privilege of getting to know him and pick his brain for the time it took to get him to the hotel and a few days later, back to the airport. He was quite a man and became one of my all time heroes.

> "Most people want the successes in life, but not failures, Get over it!"

However, I don't believe Mr. Hills quote. My experience shows me that very few ever submit again to failure. In fact, history is replete with countless examples of just the opposite. I believe some people become rich and become arrogant fat cats. They make a lot of money, but they forget about altruism, about true service to humanity, about giving, about loving, about caring.

The secret of riches is more than just the collection of dollars. It's about being a minister of encouragement to people who have less than you and using your money for good. Some people say rich people are thieves, which is not really true. Some rich people are winners in every sense of the word, but some and the opposite of what Napoleon Hill speaks about.

Also, it needs to be noted that money is not the root of all evil -- the bible says that *the love of money* is the root of all evil, the idolatry of money is the root of evil.

Rich people can buy a lot of turkeys at Thanksgiving. Rich people can build a house of worship. Rich people can fund a library. Money used for good is good.

Are there any failures in life, or are there simply lessons to be learned?

Inspire Chiropractic

Yes, there are failures in life, but the successful among us use our failures as stepping stones to growth, as lessons to be learned. There is a well known saying that tells us that within every failure resides the seed of a greater or equivalent success.

Our society in general frowns upon failure which I believe is a huge mistake. Failures are inevitable, but the winners among us get up one more time than they are knocked down.

> "Winners always persist and those who never seem to make it happen generally quit – far too early. They wear out, get frustrated and give up. My feeling is that when there is no way – find a way, but never, ever, give up."

Are there failures? Yes. Does there have to be failures? Of course, it is the one of the yin and yang's of life – the opposite of success. The issue is how one frames any failure that happens. Personally I use my failures as a reference and a lesson.

If you fail at something – let's say a spelling test – it doesn't mean you're a bad person and that you are a failure as a person. It simply means you failed a test, probably because you weren't prepared, you didn't put in your time, you didn't do your homework, or you were not a good speller.

Most people want the successes in life, but not failures, Get over it! Failures happened and will always happen. Just learn to handle them and move on. You will love the end results. And, but the way, fear of failure helps create the very kinds of failures you are attempting to avoid.

Can you share with us some failures you've encountered in your journey and what lessons they taught you?

In the beginning I failed financially, I lived on credit cards, I was always in debt. Then I read *The Richest Man in Babylon* by George Clason. This great staple of prosperity consciousness taught me to start saving 10% of everything I earned, and no matter what I had to do to attempt to live on the 90% of what I earned.

In the beginning, I saved pennies, then dollars, then tens of

Dr. Larry Markson

dollars, then thousands of dollars. That's how I became rich financially; by saving my money and living on 90%.

If people will learn the laws of financial success that Napoleon Hill speaks about in his book, and they modify and adapt their behaviors accordingly the result will be success.

Napoleon Hill talks about the importance of a mastermind group. Could you share with us what your ultimate mastermind group would be, from people both living and dead?

First, let me tell you that this is the principle I have used in my own life to accumulate the modicum of success that I have attained. I always surround myself with people of like mind who want to encourage me and support me and lead me and help me and guide me and love me and hold me up to the light.

Since reading Think and Grow Rich there has never been a time that I have not been a part of a mastermind group. I had one in Markson Management, in The Master Circle and I am engaged in one right now.

Masterminding is an essential component of creating success. The object is to surround yourself with like-minded people, people who are in total harmony with the concepts, visions and purposes of the group. This creates a collective consciousness that is synergistic in nature and it activates the Laws of Attraction that actually creates the success that is sought.

Napoleon Hill says a mastermind consists of two or more people who are working in harmony. That means two people working together have the same energy, power as four people and nine people working together have the same output of energy field as eighty one.

Utilizing The Mastermind Principle has been one of my personal keys to success.

In *Think & Grow Rich*, Napoleon Hill lists thirteen steps to riches. Those steps are as follows: desire, faith, auto-suggestion, specialized knowledge, imagination, organized planning, decision, persistence, power of the mastermind, mystery of sex transmutation, the subconscious mind, the brain, and the sixth sense. Of these steps, which are a few

Inspire Chiropractic

of your favorite principles?

To me number one ingredient of success is decisiveness. Decisiveness means the ability to make an instant and quick decision, not only from you bank of knowledge, but also from using your intuition, feelings and the sense of being naturally right.

I learned about the power of decisiveness, by observing over 25,000 chiropractors and other business people in my career. The observation of their behaviors has led me to believe without doubt that decisive people create greater successes. Eighty percent of the time they are right and 20% of their decisions turn out wrong. Likewise, those who are indecisive and weigh all the balances, over and over again, usually end up being 50% right and 50% wrong.

I also love Napoleon Hill's writing on persistence. Persist until you get it done is one of my mottos. Winners always persist and those who never seem to make it happen generally quit – far too early. They wear out, get frustrated and give up. My feeling is that when there is no way – find a way, but never, ever, give up.

Hill goes on to say that before the steps can be put into practice, you have to clear the three enemies out of your mind—indecision, doubt, and fear.

I think that he talks about procrastination, which is the killer of dreams. To me, procrastination represents having a poor self-image. It means putting off until tomorrow what you should have and would have and might have done today. It means "I don't have self-confidence. I don't have courage. I sit on a couch. I'm lazy. I'm late." All of those contra-survival values and actions with regard to success and a good self-image.

Decisiveness is on the top end, and at the bottom end, 180 degrees apart, is procrastination. Those are the two that jump out every day to me.

Fear is the number one enemy. All people want to put their foot on the gas and go forward and have more. They want more love. They want to be thinner. They want to be more beautiful. They want to have more money. They want to have more vacations. They want everything to be perfect. Everybody wants to go. On the other hand, they put their foot on the brake pedal of success

Dr. Larry Markson

because they have doubt and fear. They're afraid to do something for fear that they will either fail at it or not be good at it and feel worse about themselves than they already do.

Fear cannot be discussed in any great detail in this kind of interview. There's simply not enough time of space. I will tell you though that international best-selling author of the Chicken Soup of the Soul series, Mark Victor Hansen says F.E.A.R. is an acronym meaning False - Evidence – Appearing - Real.

In other words, we believe some things, which were taught to us by our mothers and fathers and teachers and preachers when we were young, that are not true, but we believe them to be true and we act on them as of they are true. For instance, the concept that a woman's place is in the home is clearly not true, but for years and years that was the conventional wisdom.

And because of that belief, many smart and talented women were never given the opportunities that would allow them to build the careers that they might have had.

Another false belief is that rich people are thieves. I know many rich people that are clearly not thieves of any kind. They are warm, loving, ultra-generous and good people, yet they are labeled with a mantra that is old fashioned and not true at all.

That brings us to the end of my key questions. Do you have any parting words of advice for us?

Here is some advice that I have passed on to my own children. I told them that top become successful, healthy, and happy, they should program their minds to create whatever it is they wanted in life.

The first step would be to do a stand-up, out-loud, strong and positive affirmation each and every day. Then I told them to do meditate regularly to take them out of their left brains where fear resides and utilize the power of the right brain, the right brain of creation. Finally, I told my children to be the best goal setters they know how to be, to write down what they want and when they want it, what are they going to do to get it and how the achievement of their goal will be of benefit them?

I believe that either you tell the universe exactly what it is that you want, or the universe tells you what you're going to get,

Inspire Chiropractic

which usually means the leftovers.

Lastly, I would reinforce that they were born to be successful and that no omnipotent power of the universe sponsors failures and that success, happiness, prosperity and love are choices of lifestyle and that they are more than capable of having it all.

Thank you.

>You may reach Dr. Larry Markson at:
>www.thecabinexperience.com

Dr. Larry Markson

NOTES:

Chapter 9

DR. JOHN F. DEMARTINI
Behavioral Specialist, Educator and Author

"As I began to read Think and Grow Rich, my inner sense resonated with its inspiring principles. It made great sense to me. It was practical and I could implement its principles immediately into my life. I made it almost a daily read."
-Dr. John F. Demartini

Today, Dr Demartini travels over 360 days a year to over 56 countries, where he shares his research and findings across the globe. He is the author of over forty books, published in 23 different languages. He has produced over 50 CDs and DVDs covering subjects such as personal development, relationships, wealth, education, chiropractic and business. He has created over 72 different courses, the most advanced of them is a 21-year correspondence course. Each program is designed to assist the individual to empower and activate leadership and potential in all the seven areas of their life.

Notes from the editors:

I continue to remember attending a private chiropractic seminar, where the presenter began to play a motion picture. Immediately, the film grabbed my attention. Then, Dr. John Demartini

Dr. John F. Demartini

appeared, speaking about the Law of Attraction. I was overjoyed to see him a part of this movie.

That was a few years ago. Today, most of you have heard of the smash hit, *The Secret*. Now, Dr. Demartini has expanded his life-changing principles and coaching by becoming a sensational movie star! He has appeared in many other films since *The Secret*.

> "So, everyone has their unique form of wealth or richness and the hierarchy of their values will determine and dictate its form."
>
> – Dr. John F. Demartini

He worked unwaveringly with us on this book and the truth is I could not keep up with him. In fact, he spent his Christmas Eve last year looking over this interview! Dr. John Demartini is the real deal. In this exclusive interview, you will see what I mean. Therefore, I invite you in to learn how Dr. John Demartini got inspired by the philosophy of Napoleon Hill, which enabled him to soar to the top.

-Dr. Matt Hammett

Dr. Trish Hammett interviewing Dr. John Demartini:

Tell us how you were first introduced to Napoleon Hill's *Think and Grow Rich*?

I was first introduced to Napoleon Hill's classic book *Think and Grow Rich* in 1978, when I was 23 years young. I was just about to enter into my freshman year at the Texas Chiropractic College, happened to go into a bookstore in Houston and came upon it. I immediately loved it. It was just one of those books I was inspired to buy. I bought it and the *Laws of Success* also by Napoleon Hill at the same time.

How did the book and the philosophies influence your life?

As I began to read *Think and Grow Rich*, my inner sense resonated with its inspiring principles. It made great sense to me. It was practical and I could implement its principles immediately into my life. I made it almost a daily read. I have

Inspire Chiropractic

read it over and over again many times through the years. I have incorporated it into my daily life.

You are very well known within the Chiropractic community. For the one or two people out there who aren't familiar with you and your work, can you tell us about your background in chiropractic?

As I stated before, I attended Texas Chiropractic College and graduated in May of 1982. I opened up my first practice in Houston, Texas on October 12th of that same year. My initial practice facility was expanded 9 months later, and then again 9 months after that. I eventually employed five doctors and seven support staff and practiced out of a 5,000 square foot office. I was blessed to be able to serve many thousands of clients. In 1984 was asked to speak at the Parker Seminars in Dallas and so my professional speaking and consulting services were added on top of my practice hours. In 1986 I moved my office to the 52nd floor of a tall prestigious building in uptown Houston and continued my speaking and consulting services for chiropractors and other professionals through North America while practicing part time. Since then I have continuously expanded my professional speaking career, which I now do full time. Today, I travel the world researching, writing and teaching.

In *Think and Grow Rich*, the publisher's preface says, "riches cannot always be measured in money." We would like to hear your thoughts on that statement and your own personal definition of what it means to be rich.

Every human being has a set of priorities or a set of values that they live their life by. I call this set their hierarchy of values. Whatever is highest on their values list is where they are most inspired, disciplined, empowered and wealthiest or richest. Whatever is lower on their list of values is where they are typically not as organized or focused and not as empowered or wealthy. Therefore, the hierarchy of their values dictates their financial destiny. Everybody has a different set of values. They are like individual fingerprints. For a person with a high value on family, their wealth will be in the form of their relationships with their beautiful family members. For a person who has a high value on business, their wealth will be in the form of business entrepreneurial adventures. For a person who has a high value on saving cash, their wealth will be in the form of lots of cash. So, everyone has their unique form of wealth or richness and the

Dr. John F. Demartini

hierarchy of their values will determine and dictate its form. We are all rich. Today, in many parts of the world common social values often associate richness primarily with money. But true richness comes in many forms and in all seven areas of life: spiritually, mentally, vocationally, financially, family, socially and physically. I do believe everyone can empower and develop wealth or riches in all those areas, but, certainly and particularly in the cash area. But, whatever area you value the most, this is where your richness will emerge most.

Do you feel that being rich and being successful is the same thing?

I measure each individual's successes and achievements according to their unique set or hierarchy of values. Whatever is highest on their values is where they are most disciplined, reliable and focused. This is what they identify themselves as most. In their lower values they tend to procrastinate, hesitate, and frustrate. Whenever they set goals that are congruent with their highest values, they tend to achieve them. Whenever they set goals that are not congruent with their highest values they tend not to achieve them. Their greatest achievements and successes will be in accordance with their hierarchy of values. I consider people successful when they live congruently with their highest values. This is when they feel the most fulfilled and inspired. This is when they feel the richest. When saving and investing money is highest on their values then they show their successes and achievements by becoming financially rich.

With your Breakthrough Experience, I know you have some very valuable tools that someone could use regarding their value system to increase their riches. Would you like to comment on that?

Inspire Chiropractic

> "Everyone's wisdom soars once they know what their values are and begin to set realistic goals that are congruent with them so that they can develop a new belief and confidence in themselves by achieving successfully their own true objectives."

When I began reading *Think and Grow Rich*, I was already reading books on and attending classes in personal development. That is probably why I resonated so much with its principles. I have dedicated my life to self-mastery now for the last 36+ years. So when I came across the book, I immediately incorporated some of its principles into my life. In the late 1980's I created a personal and professional development seminar program that I felt certain chiropractors and other professionals could truly benefit by. I called this unique program *The Breakthrough Experience*. I have now been able to share this amazing program with more than a quarter of a million people in 56 countries across the world. There are certain fundamental principles that people can incorporate and apply that will cause their lives to unfold in magnificent and fulfilling ways. Some of the principles I share today are still based on Napoleon Hill's original principles outlined in *Think and Grow Rich* .

I've heard you speak before where you comment on how you would hear a chiropractor say, "You know, I wish I could be more successful, like so and so down the street." Yet, their values don't match the results they are comparing themselves to, i.e. they value family vs. money. I've heard you talk about how you can help to translate those values to see where you're successful, as successful as the guy down the street is, and attract more into your life that way.

Whenever someone tells me that they're not successful and hope to someday be, I know that they are subordinating themselves to other individuals that they feel are more successful than them. I know they are comparing themselves to somebody they have placed on a pedestal. I also know that they are injecting the values of these so-called heroes into their lives

Dr. John F. Demartini

and trying to live according these other people's values, which is ultimately self-defeating. Everybody has successes – according to their own hierarchy of values. A person who is dedicated to and has a high value on watching TV as a couch potato will be more successful at watching TV than I, because I seldom watch TV, unless I'm on it, because watching TV is low on my values. Everyone has successes. They are just in forms that are according to their true values. If they compare themselves to other people, and subordinate to them, they will probably not recognize their own forms of success, because they will think they are supposed to be doing something other than what is truly high on their list of values. True achievement will occur when they are congruent with their values and they set goals that match who they truly are. It is then that they get to see, recognize and honor their own value system, and come to know their own magnificent successes and achievements.

Moving onto another concept, in *Think and Grow Rich*, Napoleon Hill includes the following quote, "A peculiar thing about the secret of riches is that those who once acquire it and use it, find themselves literally swept on to success with little effort and never again submit to failure." We'd like to hear your thoughts on that statement.

Because I define everyone's success and achievement according to their hierarchy of values, I consider everyone a success once they recognize this. People live according to those values at all times. They just don't recognize that they are doing this when they inject the values of someone they subordinate to into our lives. They think they are not succeeding or achieving, but in fact, they are. They just think they aren't because they are comparing themselves to others with a different set of values. When they think they are supposed to be living according to other people's values, they become frustrated. It is unrealistic to expect yourself to live successfully outside your own true values. As Emerson said, "envy is ignorance and imitation is suicide." Everyone's wisdom soars once they know what their values are and begin to set realistic goals that are congruent with them so that they can develop a new belief and confidence in themselves by achieving successfully their own true objectives. The more congruent they become the more certainty they develop and the more they catapult even further achievements. They can just keep building successes upon successes. I call it momentum building. When they achieve they tend to reward themselves for

Inspire Chiropractic

being congruent with themselves, and then they tend to achieve even more.

> "I probably have the largest collection of words of power and affirmation statements than anyone else on earth and I say many of them daily to myself."

How do you feel the Law of Attraction plays into this concept?

Everyone lives according to whatever they believe will help them fulfill their highest values. So, whatever is highest on their value list will dictate their selective perceptions and actions. They will tend to see anything that will help them support their highest values in their environment. They will also tend to act in a way that will support their higher values. And they will tend to retain any information that will help them accomplish or fulfill their highest values. I call these reality filters simply "attention surplus order," "intention surplus order" and "retention surplus order". Whatever is lower on their values, they will tend to not see, act upon, or remember. I call these "attention deficit disorder," "intention deficit disorder" and "retention deficit disorder". Whenever they are setting goals that are congruent with their highest values, they tend to see opportunities around them to help them fulfill their objectives.

> "I say that what we misperceive to be failure is simply feedback to help us to set goals that are congruent with our highest values."

They will also see these opportunities; act upon these opportunities; and retain information concerning these opportunities. What is called the Law of Attraction is simply the synchronicity of seeing, acting and retaining those things in their environment that are most congruent with their highest values. For example; a woman whose highest value is taking care of her children will see opportunities to buy things for her children and take action on those that will support her children. She will

Dr. John F. Demartini

increase the probability of achieving whatever her highest values are (her children) because of it. So, regarding the Law of Attraction, it is not just that they are attracting things into their lives as much as they are actually recognizing the synchronicities and acting upon those that are already there. They are taking advantage of them more efficiently and effectively because they are simply congruent with their most important values. People who set goals that are not aligned with their values tend not to notice these synchronicities and feel the Law of Attraction is not working for them, even though ultimately it actually is.

So, in essence, you could be attracting what you might think you want, but because it is not congruent with your values, you don't see it?

Opportunities are always around. But if these opportunities are not perceived as being aligned with what is highest on their a person's list of values, they will not recognize them, nor take advantage of them. Everyone has a biased selective attention that is constantly filtering their reality. This means that if they do not have a high value on something, they will probably overlook it. Let me give you an example. I was walking in the mall in Texas a number of years ago with a gentleman who had a net worth of about 200 million dollars. He had a high value on building wealth, obviously. As we walked and talked through the mall, I noticed the bookstore and the discovery store, while he noticed what stores were busiest and which might make great investments. Because of his hierarchy of values, which was topped off by building great wealth, and my values, which was learning the laws of the universe, we both saw two different malls. My mall contained the bookstore because I love reading and learning and because I'm a teacher, while his mall was filled with opportunities for building money and wealth. I had a high value on money, but not as high as he did. I have a higher value on learning. Therefore, I saw things about learning; he saw things about wealth building. This is a classic example of two sets of value dictating to different destinies.

What is your definition or concept of failure? Is there any such thing as failure in life?

Inspire Chiropractic

I generally don't use the term failure. I use the term feedback. I say that what we misperceive to be failure is simply feedback to help us to set goals that are congruent with our highest values. So-called failure is nothing more than a feedback mechanism to make sure that we are congruent with our highest values

> "Persistence is certainly a key to success."

and true to ourselves. I don't see that as a failure, I just see it as a homing mechanism or negative feedback loop to guide us back to our true mission. As a result the term failure doesn't mean anything else to me. I don't see how failure could actually ever occur, since, no matter what people have done in their lives, it could be seen as nothing but feedback to just move them closer to what they love doing.

Could you share with us any of these key feedbacks and what lessons you learned from them?

There have been times when I assumed something was going to happen, and then it didn't happen the way I originally imagined. Something else happened instead. I then came to realize that what did actually happen ultimately served me in even a greater way than what I previously imagined. At first, I thought what happened was a setback, but I then realized it was a step forward. The former was my illusion. The latter was my surprise. So, failures are simply labels that we give to events and actions that we have not yet seen the hidden order to. They are actually stepping-stones along the way to what we would truly love to be, do and have.

Napoleon Hill talks about the importance of a Master Mind group. Can you share with us what would make up your ideal Master Mind group if you could choose from people both living and dead?

I'm blessed to be able to hang out with those people that I would love to interact with. So, make a list of the most inspiring and empowered people in the areas of life that you would love to enhance and master and then work toward associating with them. I have Master Mind group partners all over the world and they range from politicians to world leaders, and celebrities to great minds. They are leaders in all areas of life. Anybody who is making a global difference and wants to impact the world and

Dr. John F. Demartini

leave some sort of legacy on the planet, I love hanging out with them. So they make up my Master Mind partners today. I also study the lives of the greatest beings alive today and throughout history and fill out the Demartini Method® forms on them so as to own inside myself all the traits I see inside them, so I see them as my global colleagues. Whatever you see in others you have inside yourself. Yes, even to the same degree.

Of the 13 steps to Riches that Napoleon Hill talks about, what do you consider the most important principles?

I have a slightly different language for describing some of these 13 steps, but I am a firm believer in the power of then. Those actions and goals that are highest on your value list you will be inspired from within to do, and no one will have to get you up in the morning to do them. For example; what Napoleon Hill calls desire, I call being inspired by. For that which is most meaningful, most purposeful and most important to you, you just can't wait to do. If your goals are congruent with your highest values the step he calls desire automatically emerges. We cannot wait to get up in the morning to do what we are most inspired to do. I am a firm believer in this first step. Nobody ever has to get me up in the morning to get me to teach. I love being a teacher. What he calls faith is also great. For I say that there is a magnificent hidden order in the universe. No matter what happens, it is guiding us and giving us feedback to live authentically. If you want to call that having faith in that order, then that's fine. I just call it honoring the hidden order. I am certain about that hidden order. I have been involved with studying it for over three decades. I just describe desire as actually just having certainty of action and appreciation for the magnificent hidden order of the universe. I believe that there is an inner prompting and inner guidance mechanism that guides us to fulfill what we are here to do. I love exploring that step. Of course, I love exploring them all!

I am a firm believer in saying daily affirmations or words of power and having internal conversations or what Napoleon Hill called auto-suggestion. I probably have the largest collection of words of power and affirmation statements than anyone else on earth and I say many of them daily to myself. I have enough to keep me busy literally 24 hours a day easily. I have thousands of them. So I'm a firm believer in utilizing the power of words. A few of the affirmations I have said most consistently and the

Inspire Chiropractic

longest are; *I am a genius and I apply my wisdom. I am a master of persistence and I do what it takes. I love what I do and do what I love. I am a master reader, whatever I read I retain ....*

I have also been a long-term, firm believer in developing specialized knowledge. I've read nearly 29,000 books in 275 disciplines. So I could be perceived as quite a generalist, but my specialties are human behavior, healing and the evolution of human consciousness. I love learning ways to assist people in expanding their awareness and potential. So I am constantly studying and learning. I believe that expanding my mind with specialized knowledge is one of the most important actions I can do.

Being creative with our minds and being very present while holding the image of how we would love our lives to be and what would fulfill our dreams is also vital. Our vitality is directly proportionate to the vividness of our vision.

I have literally spent thousands of hours doing organized planning. I also have additional people actually helping me in my planning process now in different sub- specialties and in different countries, because I now have so many facets to my primary work. My "State of My Mission" book, which contains my life time affirmations, goals and objectives, accomplishments and post humus biography is now over 700 pages long.

Decision making is crucial to achievement. Whatever is highest on our value is where we make the most efficient decisions, because our awareness is extremely heightened and our actions are more concise in this area. Decision making comes quickly to someone whose goals are congruent with their highest values.

Persistence is certainly a key to success. When you are doing something you love to do and you are inspired by it and you cannot wait to get up in the morning and do it, you just automatically persist at doing it. Others will call you determined and persistent, but you will just feel you are loving what you do.

I have already mentioned the importance of having a Master Mind. Hanging out with global leaders is one of the ways that you can more effectively leave global effects. If your vision of service is truly greater than your own mortal needs, one that stretches at least a thousand years into the future, then you will automatically resonate with and attract global leaders into your

Dr. John F. Demartini

life. Why not make a global difference.

Sex transmutation is at times also essential. I travel full time so I only rendezvous with my girlfriend periodically. I utilize my sexual energy by being creative with my work. When I'm very busy, often 20 hours a day, I have a very strong sexual energy transmuted into business actions and opportunities or whatever else I am doing across the world.

In the Subconscious Mind lies a hidden power. When are goals are congruent with our highest values, our conscious and our subconscious automatically become aligned and congruent. When they are we amazingly begin to manifest creatively. Most people are incongruent and their subconscious minds manifest things that their conscious minds do not always appreciate or align with. I feel I am blessed with a high degree of congruency. I tend to get pretty well whatever I set my mind to and what I want to create it in my life. Our brains are great gifts because they act as mediators between our physical world and our inspirations. They are tuning devices that allows us to tune into what our most inspired visions are. As I stated on *The Secret*, "When the voice and the vision on the inside becomes more profound and louder than all opinions on the outside, you have begun to master your life." When they do, your brain becomes highly organized and coherent and your living vitality explodes. Our brains are creative by nature.

The intuitive sixth sense acts as a feedback mechanism to make sure that we see things wholly and that we are balanced in our expectations and aligned with our highest values. I have been researching the sixth sense and teaching about the importance of it, for all these years.

You've mentioned what a lover of knowledge you are. Share with us some of the books you think are key for chiropractors to read?

I have been blessed to be able to read so much. The two books that I tell people to fill their minds with are two the volumes created by Britannica called *Syntopicon Volumes I & II*. They contain a collection of the greatest minds of the Western world over the last 2,500 years. They discuss and explore the greatest and the most universal ideas that human beings can study. I think these are two masterpieces, and I encourage all of my

Inspire Chiropractic

students to study them because of it. Those two books stand out in my mind. There are hundreds and hundreds of books that I believe are worthy. I certainly believe that reading the green books by B.J. and the blue books by D.D. are certainly advisable. By reading all the books that have been created by chiropractors over the decades and by filling our minds with great and inspiring ideas we can get in turn inspired about providing ever greater levels of healing service to the world.

At the end of the book, Napoleon Hill says that before any of these steps can be put into practice that we must clear three enemies out of our minds. He lists these as indecision, doubt and fear. Can you share with us some tools that you have used to clear these enemies out of your way?

Any time you set goals that are congruent with your highest values you will see opportunities, you will act on opportunities, and you will make decisions quickly, concisely and effectively. However, any time you set goals that are aligned with lower values, because these goals are often injected into your life as a result of you subordinating to other authorities, you tend to hesitate, procrastinate and frustrate on them. When you do, your certainty will decline, because you will tend to believe that you can't and / or you don't know. So, it is very important to set goals that are congruent with your highest values. The minute you do your fears drop, your decisions get quicker and your hesitations subside. So congruency is the most important solution to those three so-called enemies. Fear is an assumption that you are about to experience in the future through your senses or imagination, more pain than pleasure, more loss than gain, more negative than positive, or more challenge than support from someone or yourself. In actuality, the Universe never allows such an imbalance. The Universe maintains a beautiful and elegant balance of complementary opposites. Whenever we're challenged there's always support; whenever there's a negative there's always a positive; whenever there's a pain there's always a pleasure; whenever there's a loss there's always a gain; whenever the window shuts there is always a door that opens. There is no such thing as an imbalanced Universe. Fear is false evidence appearing real. It is assuming that there is going to be an imbalance, when in actuality there never is. Train your mind by looking back at your life and every moment you had something you were frightened about look for the hidden blessings in it and discover how it actually served at the moment. Find out where the other side

Dr. John F. Demartini

was at the moment you thought it was not there. Training your mind to see the balance synchronously allows you to transcend future fear based limitations. That in itself will help to increase the speed and clarity of your decisions and dissolve your concerns that create doubt.

> "Allow yourself the opportunity to be a leader. Because, when your goals are congruent with your true values, your true self, your leadership automatically emerges and electrifies the movement of other people towards great causes."

You have mentioned about having goals that are congruent with your highest values. If someone feels that they are not getting the results that they want in their life, and they realize that, it is because their goals are not congruent with their values. What has to change? Do you change your goals or your values?

They have two choices. First, they can honor their own values by setting realistic goals that match them. Any time you set goals that are not congruent with your highest values you will end up with the ABC's of negativity towards yourself: you'll be angry, you'll be aggressive, you'll be blaming, you'll feel betrayed, you'll feel critical and you'll feel challenged. But the second you set goals that are congruent, you will automatically electrify your actions and you'll move on to achieve. That is the secret of the law of attraction and accomplishment. Now, if you find that your goals are not aligned to your values and you want to change your values to match your goals, then there are the *Demartini Method of Value Determination™*, and the *Demartini Method of Value Transformation™* methods available to help you. These methods involve more than I could say in just a few lines, but they basically work by; first determining your present values, i.e. looking at exactly what your life demonstrates is important to you. This is done by looking at how you spend your time, energy and money and how you fill your space. Also where you are most disciplined and organized and what you think about most, visualize most, affirm most, converse about most, what you are inspired by most and what goals you are most consistently focused on. Second, transforming your values to match your

Inspire Chiropractic

goals is done by stacking up a long list of benefits or new associations about the values that you would love to raise on your value list. Those values that will best help you accomplish those goals. This is done by answering the question, "How will fulfilling this particular value help me fulfill my goal(s)?" By answering that question up to a thousand times can reprogram the value list and transform the priorities in your life.. Because when you have a big enough reason for doing something, you will do it- but if you don't, you won't. Many times the goals people think are important to them, aren't, because there are other objectives stacked up higher on their value list that they want to do instead. Whatever your life is demonstrating, reflects your values. So if you say you want to do something, but you're not doing it, it's because there are other things more important to you at that time. Otherwise, you would just get on and do it.

Is there a specific book of yours that you would recommend that talks more about these concepts?

Probably, the book that would match this chapter most would be *The Riches Within - Your Seven Secret Treasures* and second most would be The *Breakthrough Experience – A Revolutionary New Approach to Personal Transformation.* I think those two books would be applicable because they are addressing how to empower the seven areas of life, just as Napoleon Hill's book does. They also discuss how to determine and how to be congruent and align with your true values. I have another book on wealth building called *How to Make One Hell of a Profit and Still Get to Heaven.* This book shows you how to raise your values on wealth building, so you can build cash rich wealth base in addition to life fulfillment. In it, I show you the mechanism and the actual step-by-step procedure how to do that. And if you prefer to listen to CDs or watch DVDs in order to inspire you to action, then I have two gems that can help you build your wealth faster. These are *The Secrets to Financial Success* and *Wealth Wisdom of the Ages.*

Do you have any parting words of advice for us?

No matter what you have been through and no matter who you are, deep inside your heart, you have a yearning, a calling and an inner vision and purpose that is truly in line with your highest values. Once you tap into it and get inspired by it, amazing things will emerge in your daily life. You will see opportunities. You will act on opportunities. You will manifest things. You have inside you a great creator, and you are here to be an inspired leader for others and for the world. Give yourself permission to do something extraordinary, something amazing on planet Earth. Allow yourself not to shrink, but to shine. Allow yourself to do something that is a legacy, for not just immediate gratification, but for a long-term vision, maybe even for a millennium. Allow yourself the opportunity to be a leader. Because, when your goals are congruent with your true values, your true self, your leadership automatically emerges and electrifies the movement of other people towards great causes. So, allow yourself to be all you can be. You are great. Do not question it; go live it.

You may reach Dr. John Demartini at:
www.drdemartini.com
info@drdemartini.com

Inspire Chiropractic

NOTES

Chapter 10

DR. PATRICK GENTEMPO, Jr.
CEO of Creating Wellness Alliance
&
Chiropractic Leadership Alliance

"I fortunately grew up with a mother that taught me the principles of positive thinking, self-confidence, etc., and I think that the book expanded upon that foundation."
-Dr. Patrick Gentempo, Jr.

Dr. Patrick Gentempo, Jr. is co-founder and CEO of the Chiropractic Leadership Alliance (CLA) which has over 8,000 chiropractic clients on 6 continents. He is an internationally renowned visionary, lecturer, business leader and author. As one of the largest draws in chiropractic today, he is considered to be unmatched in his ability to integrate the philosophy, science, clinical practice and business of chiropractic without contradiction. Over the past 20 years, Dr. Gentempo has mesmerized audiences with his vision of world leadership of healthcare in a chiropractic model. He has received numerous awards of the highest level within the chiropractic profession. Dr. Gentempo has also provided testimony to the White House Commission on Complimentary and Alternative Medicine and in 2007 was inducted into the Wellness Hall of Fame.

Inspire Chiropractic

He has appeared on many popular television and radio programs. Dr. Gentempo also currently serves as CEO of the Creating Wellness Alliance (CWA). Creating Wellness has hundreds of affiliated chiropractic wellness offices throughout North America, Europe and New Zealand. Through a revolutionary new chiropractic service model and economic model, Creating Wellness is building a sophisticated international consumer brand of chiropractic in the context of wellness.

Notes from the editors:

Some of us have had the privilege of attending one of the most exciting seminars in chiropractic, *Total Solutions*. This is a memorable event for any chiropractor, entrepreneur, or leader. Created by Dr. Patrick Gentempo, Jr., this seminar teaches us how to apply the philosophy of chiropractic and success, as well as presenting insights from some of the world-renowned experts, such as Nathaniel Branden, bestselling author of *The Psychology of Self-Esteem*.

> "I think that a willingness to make mistakes and a willingness to fail is the key to growth. There is no question about it."
> – Dr. Patrick Gentempo, Jr.

As I write this introduction to the interview, on the wall is a photograph of my wife and me climbing to the top of a telephone pole during one of the *Total Solution* seminars we attended a few years ago. For most of you, that may not seem like a big deal. However, try doing it in the middle of December, in Colorado, while wearing a pair of oversized boots that could fit Shaquille O'Neal! Talk about the application of faith!

Take a moment to be mesmerized by the mind and words of Dr. Patrick Gentempo, Jr. and learn how he applied Napoleon Hill's philosophy from *Think and Grow Rich*.

-Dr. Matt Hammett

Dr. Trish Hammett interviewing Dr. Patrick Gentempo:

Dr. Patrick Gentempo, Jr.

Our first question is how and when were you first introduced to Napoleon Hill's *Think & Grow Rich*?

I discovered *Think & Grow Rich* when I was in practice in the early to mid-1980s. I was a member of *Markson Management Services*, and it was there that I saw a presentation on *Think and Grow Rich*, bought the book and read it. The rest is history.

How has the book's philosophies influenced your life?

I fortunately grew up with a mother that taught me the principles of positive thinking, self-confidence, etc., and I think that the book expanded upon that foundation. I am a little bit different from many other people that were shown a completely new light by the book and those who rewired themselves as a result. I think *Think and Grow Rich*, instead, enhanced a foundation that was already built into and nurtured in me.

Tell us about your background in chiropractic.
I graduated chiropractic school in 1983, and practiced from 1983 until 1991. During the time I was in practice, I started developing diagnostic technology for chiropractors with a partner, Dr. Christopher Kent.

Once I started to offer this technology to the chiropractic profession, I realized that the machine alone did not achieve results in a practice. It is the *who*, or rather the identity, of the person using the machine that achieved results. Consequently, we started creating personal development, practice development, and business consulting type programs for chiropractors that integrated with the technology. We built what we call the Chiropractic Leadership Alliance, which now provides a variety of products and services to the profession including a transformational boot camp, called Total Solution. Our boot camp has created success with many chiropractors. The Alliance also includes our monthly *On Purpose* audio program. The program focuses on the philosophy, science, and art of chiropractic. In fact, we just celebrated its 15th anniversary.

From there, we have evolved into the *Creating Wellness Alliance*, which now offers a business brand and structure for chiropractors to become Creating Wellness Centers.

In *Think & Grow Rich*, the publisher's preface states that

Inspire Chiropractic

riches cannot always be measured in money. We would like to hear your thoughts on that statement, as well as your personal idea and definition of being rich.

Well, I think that being rich is very often a state of mind. I could best illustrate this with a true story I just heard yesterday. A German billionaire ran into serious financial difficulties and as a result, threw himself in front of a train and killed himself. Now, for somebody like that maybe even with all his difficulties, he would have been able to lead a millionaire's life. Yet, the concept to him of failing or losing his billionaire status was so overwhelming that he decided to throw himself in front of a train. What that tells me is that this man's identity was tied to his monetary status. Now, I am not so naïve to think that monetary status is not a part of one's experience, self-perception, or identity. Of course, I think this is because money is often used as a yardstick to measure certain aspects of your efficacy in your career as a human being. Unless you have values, in your life that are worth living for, whether you have money or not, you do not really have much of a life.

I was thinking about this not that long ago. My quote is, "That the best thing about life is the fact that we have one." I think that is where it starts, and from there everything else grows. In other words, if you have gratitude or an appreciation for being alive, that grows to gratitude, for having your health, for the people that are in your life that you love and care about, and that grows to gratitude for the things that you love and care about. Therefore, I think most people, if not all, need some degree of monetary success in order to be able to take care of themselves.

Nathaniel Branden is a brilliant psychotherapist who is the godfather of self-esteem. He defines self-esteem as the ability to be able to cope with the challenges of life and the sense of being worthy of happiness. Not everybody wants to be a billionaire or even a millionaire; however, everybody aspires to produce a certain amount of monetary sustenance to live life on a certain level. This even applies to somebody who goes into a monastery and says, "I really don't want much material things in my life, but I'm still going to have to provide a certain effort every day to earn my keep. I have to be fed and sheltered, and that still requires some effort on my part. I have to provide some kind of work to earn that." On the other hand, someone else could say, "I have the ability and the desire to earn extraordinary wealth." That statement, may very well define their career goals.

Dr. Patrick Gentempo, Jr.

Nevertheless, money is just one dimension of a multidimensional life.

It is a very complex subject when you start looking at the interplay between your own health and fitness, your relationships, your career, your financial life, and your spiritual life. All these things have complex interactions and the sum total of them make up what your life is. If a human being does not understand the interaction between these various aspects of their life, or if they have contradictions in the values between these various aspects of their life, it will create a breakdown.

> "You sculpt yourself in a certain way, and you are never going to go back or

What is the relationship between being rich and being successful? Are they the same thing or are they different?

If I am assuming that you mean monetarily rich and successful, I do not know how to answer that question because it is a relative term. Rich for some people might mean they have $100,000 in the bank and for other people $100,000 in the bank might mean that they are on the verge of being destitute. It is really a self-imposed, self-defined state. I think it probably goes back to what I said earlier. When you say successful, there are categories of success, i.e. health and fitness, spirituality, relationships, monetarily, etc. Are you successful in those areas? These are dimensions of success. Are you rich in those areas? I think it is kind of the same thing. To me, it is a matter of the sum total of all the dimensions of your life as well as the individual components of it. I know a great many people who are very rich monetarily and very poor spiritually or in their relationships, and vice versa. I know some people who do not have much money but they are very rich in their relationships or they are very fit and healthy. I know some people, friends of mine, that work on Wall Street with high-stress jobs and make millions and millions of dollars, but their health is terrible. To me, what good is all that money if you do not feel good? So to me, there are many categories of one's life, only one being money, and I believe that you can ascribe the terms, or concepts, of rich or successful to each of those categories.

In *Think & Grow Rich*, Napoleon Hill includes the following quote, "a peculiar thing about this secret of riches is that

Inspire Chiropractic

those who once acquire it and use it, find themselves literally swept on to success but with little effort and they never again submit to failure." We would like to hear your thoughts on that statement.

I think what this means is that once you acquire a certain level of achievement, you now have identified, or validated a certain sense of your self-worth and your capacities for achievement. You have changed your frame of reference; you cannot go back, retreat or devolve into a former lower state of existence. In my mind, this is related to the Darwinian concept of evolution, which says that over time the human species and all species on the planet evolve into stronger, better, more adaptable members of the planet. I think evolution is also a process in the individual. As they work toward improvement and as they evolve, they change the state of who they are as well as their perception of who they are. Therefore, they are never going back, because nobody wants to devolve.

I am not saying that reversals do not happen to people, because they do. Sometimes I have seen people on top of the world who are dealt some type of a serious blow and they can lose it. This is a horrible example, but somebody who is successful in their life, their career is going well, they have a good spouse, and great kids; they are living a whole life that is a dream. Everything is going right. However, let us say that a member or some members of the family are tragically killed in an accident. Well, that can take away their motivation and they could devolve back into something that was a lower level of existence that predates what they had achieved in their life. Further, I know of people that have faced those tragedies, fallen down to lower levels of function, and then recovered and overcame it, by fighting their way back. These are not unusual stories. You can find them everywhere.

I think that in the end what this is talking about is that as you are self-made in your life, you sculpt yourself in a certain way, and you are never going to go back or devolve to where you once were.

Do you believe that there are any failures in life or are they simply lessons to be learned?

Dr. Patrick Gentempo, Jr.

I think it is both. I think you can fail and you can learn from the failure. I am not of the school that there are no failures, only lessons learned; I think that is a cop out, and an easy way to accept failure. Failure is a waste if you did not learn from it. I do believe that an individual can fail forward, and that failure does not have to mean that you go backwards.

How do you define the term failure? I think failure is the lack of achieving an important goal. You set out to do something and you failed at doing it. For example, if you die from heart failure, what did you learn from it? You are dead. If you are a pilot and you fail to land the airplane properly, people die. So I cannot subscribe to the idea of failures only being lessons. Sometimes failure might mean that you are not alive any more. There is a real thing called failure and if you are lucky enough to survive it, you can learn from it.

> "Autosuggestion and faith go hand in hand because if you say to yourself, "I can, I will, I must," as your autosuggestion, then your desire is translated into a psychological state that says, "I can.""

Can you share with us any examples of failures from your own life and what you learned from them?

Oh, my God, there are so many. As I like to tell people, as much as I am perceived as successful in my industry, and I am, at the same time, for every good decision I have made, there has probably been four bad ones. I think that a willingness to make mistakes and a willingness to fail is the key to growth. There is no question about it. Obviously, you want to learn from your mistake and you want to make sure that you do not repeat them.

I have had failed relationships in my past, but I have learned from them. So now, I have great relationships. I have had failures in my career where I have lost millions of dollars investing in ideas that did not work, but I learned from them. I am quite sure that my failures are not even close to over yet, but I am committed to working through them to get to higher levels of success. In just about every dimension of my life at some point in time, I have failed. Fortunately, I have been able to overcome those failures and to build a life that I am very proud of and that I am very happy to live.

Napoleon Hill talks about the importance of a mastermind group. If you were to put together your ideal mastermind group from people both living and dead, who would be in your group?

I think the real question is, who the people I find most influential are, or whose wisdom I respect the most. I would first say my mother. She has always given and continues to give me good ideas. Actually, I would include both my mom and dad. Ayn Rand, the philosopher. I would include D.D. and B.J. Palmer, the discoverer and developer of chiropractic. I would put in my partner, Christopher Kent. My wife, Lori, certainly I am talking with her about ideas all the time. I would put in Nathaniel Branden, whom I mentioned earlier. Aristotle. The Dalai Lama, I think might have some interesting input here. I guess that is probably a big enough group.

In *Think & Grow Rich*, Napoleon Hill lists thirteen steps to riches. He talks about desire, faith, autosuggestion, specialized knowledge, etc. Of these steps, which are your favorite principles and why? Is there one, two or three that you feel are more influential?

I think they are all important. The reason they are steps is that they are all a part of it. I think desire is obviously a key step. Autosuggestion, I think, is a highlight for sure. Imagination has to be there. Then organized planning is another one I would tick off, followed by persistence.

If I were to try look at it in a sequential way, they build upon each other; desire, autosuggestion, imagination, planning, organization, and persistence. First, without desire you are lost. Then I think that autosuggestion is important because once you have the desire, if you are telling yourself that you are not capable, you are lost. Autosuggestion and faith go hand in hand because if you say to yourself, "I can, I will, I must," as your autosuggestion, then your desire is translated into a psychological state that says, "I can." Then imagination says that I need creative ideas to make whatever what I want into a reality. However, many people live in imagination land and they do not plan and organize. You are dead if you don't do that. Your vision never becomes reality if you do not have organized planning. Finally, persistence is necessary because anything that you want to do is always harder than what most people

Dr. Patrick Gentempo, Jr.

think.

Therefore, if you have desire, positive autosuggestion, good imagination, organized planning and persistence, I think you will succeed.

Napoleon Hill then says that before any of those steps can be put into practice, we have to clear three enemies out of our mind. He lists those as indecision, doubt, and fear. Can you share with us some tools that you have used to clear those enemies out of your way?

For indecision, the tool is just to understand that you have to make decisions. If an individual is going to lead, they must make decisions and sometimes those are hard decisions. I have a saying, "Leaders are people who make hard decisions so everyone benefits." Indecision, though, will only lead to entropy. If you are not making decisions and moving in a direction or towards organization, you end up going into disassociation and entropy. Being conscious of how important decisions are is the tool.

I'll catch myself in indecision, because I am somebody who can get very analytical sometimes. I can be shopping for a camera and I might find myself lost for an hour, trying to decide between one camera versus another on minor details. Suddenly I'll recognize that the time that I spent making this decision is worth more than the transaction. Then I will say, "Just make a decision now." That is just an example. That's a $400 camera: a minor decision. When you are making a decision about who you want to marry, well then, you had better take more than an hour to make that decision. You determine how much time you want to take to make the decision based on the importance of the decision.

Doubt is an interesting thing. There are up cycles and down cycles. When things are going well for an individual, they are in this upward spiral and doubt and fear do not really come around very often. Doubt and fear come around when things are turning against you and, of course, that is the times when you can least afford them in your life. I think the same tool is used for both doubt and fear. I think this tool is a disciplined process of orchestrating your mindset by doing your affirmations in the morning, and looking at your goals.

Inspire Chiropractic

Doubt and fear exist in the mid-brain. They are fight-flight mechanisms. Vision, purpose, goals, imagination, exist in the neocortex. The way to overcome doubt and fear is to put yourself into neocortical function versus mid-brain function. The way that you do this is by looking at what you want to achieve, by self-affirming, looking at your goals, your visions, and purpose, etc., and by being grateful for things in your life. You cannot simultaneously have doubt and fear while you are thinking about your purpose and goals. Therefore, if you recognize that you have doubt and fear, you have to start thinking about your purpose, goals and what you are grateful for -- suddenly, doubt and fear will just evaporate.

Could you share with us some of your favorite books and authors and reasons you believe those books and authors are worthy of us getting to know.

Easily the most important book I have ever read in my life is *Atlas Shrugged* by Ayn Rand. The reason that that book is so important is because it defined the moral virtue of capitalism, not just in economic terms but also in terms of one's inalienable right to life, liberty, and the pursuit of happiness. *Atlas Shrugged* gave me permission to enjoy success in life without having to experience any requisite guilt. It showed me the moral virtue of production and it gave clarity to a sense of life and intellectual concepts that have served me in very powerful ways.

Do you have any parting words of advice for us?

Parting words of advice? *Think & Grow Rich!*

Thank you.

You may reach Dr. Patrick Gentempo, Jr. at:
www.subluxation.com

Dr. Patrick Gentempo, Jr.

NOTES:

Chapter 11

DR. TEDD KOREN
Developer of Koren Specific Technique
Fought and beat the Federal Government and
Quack Busters

"You see, it does not matter what you have gone through, (and you are going to go through many tough things in life), you have to learn from it, and grow, and not get bitter."
-Dr. Tedd Koren

Dr. Tedd Koren is the most widely read Doctor of Chiropractic in the world today with over 50 million of his popular scientifically referenced patient education brochures in distribution. Koren Publications (www.korenpublications.com) also publishes chiropractic books, posters, office forms, stickers and childhood vaccination materials. Dr. Koren produces a monthly

"Napoleon Hill always tells you to keep your eyes open and do not stop learning. Do not stop if you believe in something. We have to keep going."

– Dr. Tedd Koren

Dr. Tedd Koren

newsletter for patients (www.patientnewsletter.com). Dr. Koren is the developer of Koren Specific Technique, a breakthrough in patient care.

Notes from the editors:

Can you envision what it would be like to work hard at your chosen profession, while also helping your colleagues to build a better future? Imagine inspiring millions of people to seek the services of your profession and one day receiving a terrible letter from someone who wanted to dissolve your profession and you! That is exactly what happened to the remarkable Dr. Tedd Koren.

What was going through his mind when he read this horrible message? How would he, as one person, take on this new evil and lead his profession into the millennium? What kind of leader and visionary would this person need to be? What thought processes would this person need? What kind of philosophy and strength would this person have to posses to accomplish this?

In the next few pages, I invite you in on an exclusive interview with Dr. Tedd Koren to learn how he used Napoleon Hill's philosophy to become one of the world's greatest successes in chiropractic and how he defeated the U.S. Government and the Quack Busters. You will want to read this interview more than once in order to pull out the gems that will help you to defeat your fears and accomplish your goals!

-Dr. Matt Hammett

Dr. Trish Hammett interviewing Dr. Tedd Koren:

The first question we would like to ask is how and when were you first introduced to Napoleon Hill's *Think and Grow Rich*?

Well I read the book many years ago. I thought Napoleon Hill was one of the first people to talk about the power of the mind in

Inspire Chiropractic

modern settings and about applying it to things as mundane as having a successful life financially. This was a bit of a radical thing to do at that time. I think at the time people were just limiting that kind of stuff to spirituality and feeling good about other people, instead he was saying, "Let's bring it down to earth." I think that is a very valuable lesson for everybody- to make things practical.

Can you give us an overview of how this book and its philosophies have influenced your life? I know personally that I am curious regarding the things that you have gone through in fighting Quack Busters and your other legal battles. Have you used some of these principles in calling in and reigning in the resources to do the work that you have done?

We were fighting the Federal government before the Quack Busters. I never wanted to be a political kind of guy. I just wanted to write patient literature. I was a teacher, suddenly I am into this political world, and it was nasty. People that I had respected in the profession, leaders in schools and organizations that I looked up to, turned their back on us. They essentially said, "It's your fight. Goodbye." Although, not everybody, there were some notable exceptions, but I learned more than I wanted to know. I think that is part of the growing up process. Napoleon Hill always tells you to keep your eyes open and do not stop learning. Do not stop if you believe in something. We have to keep going. This is not something that we can turn our backs on, even if other people are turning their backs on it. It was tough, and it was not easy, but we wound up finding a wonderful attorney who turned the whole thing around for us. After that, we felt like we had to give back. I felt very grateful, and for that reason, we started the Foundation for Health Choice. That is going to be the vehicle through which we are fighting the Quack Busters.

As things grow, you have to keep open. We could have gotten very bitter and paranoid. My attorney warned me about that happening. He said, "I don't want you to get paranoid. This is not against you personally. This is not personal; this is just what is happening in the world today." I never took it personal. I always try to look at the bigger picture. You have to look for the people that are truly loving, caring and are more open. Through all of this, we have found some wonderful people who supported us.

Dr. Tedd Koren

Can you briefly tell us about your background in the chiropractic profession for those who may not be as familiar with your career?

Well I started practicing after I graduated as Valedictorian of Sherman College. At that time, I also helped to found the Pennsylvania College of Chiropractic, also known as ADIO. I began to teach and write for the journal, and things rather snowballed. After a while, I began to be noticed, and I became noticed by the bad guys, the Quack Busters.

"You need to follow carefully, and not follow anything more than what feels right to you. You have to look within, because we can be fooled in our lives."

Before that, I was not sure if the literature I had written would be successful. I felt chiropractors were mostly only caring about low back pain. I came out with a line of brochures, (I believe there were 36 titles), that were about asthma, allergies, subluxations and wellness, ear infections, menstrual pain, etc. Traditionally it was not known by the public that people who have these problems should go to chiropractors. I wanted to do something that could really help. My fear was that there would not be any people interested in that kind of patient education. Fortunately, that gamble paid off and we wound up selling 45 or 50 million brochures and distributing them all over the world, even publishing in Australia and distributing to Canada and many other countries.

Things just grew. I did not know what would happen. I just did not want to loose my car. (I had decided if I could not pay the bank note, I would have to sell my car.) Fortunately, I did not have to sell my car. People liked the material so I started writing more and more. Then I started getting involved with vaccinations because my son was born. I never looked back. I never questioned it, because it seemed like right thing to do. You have to follow your instincts and your heart. You have to be true to yourself. It's a cliché, but you really have to do what feels right to you. You cannot fake it. People can try to fake it. People can make money and not be true to themselves, but they are not going to be happy.

Inspire Chiropractic

In Think and Grow Rich, the publishers preface says that riches cannot always be measured in money; we would like to hear your thoughts on that statement as well as your idea and definition of being rich?

Well there is an old Jewish saying, "Whether you are rich or poor, its good to have money." This essentially means that money can make you comfortable. There is no doubt about it. Studies even show that wealthier people tend to be healthier and happier. So I am not going to give the pie in the sky answer and say, "Oh no, you don't need money for happiness at all." It *can* be an essential factor. I have known and know many people, however, who live depressed miserable lives, but are loaded with money. They are uncultured, limited and have very little concept about life and health. I even know chiropractors like that- people who might have had a lot of money, but I would not want to spend a minute or two in their company. We have to realize money is one thing, but it does not mean you will have a good marriage. You cannot buy a happy marriage. You cannot buy children who love you- you cannot even buy a dog that will love you. You cannot do any of that with money alone. Take Shakespeare, for example. Shakespeare always had one eye on the cash register. He wrote plays that he knew would be successful. He created poetry, literature, novels and characters that were incredible entertainment. At the same time, he was aware of the money aspect and that he could not separate one from the other.

Do you have a personal motto for success?

You know, when I was a kid, I came from what I feel, was a very dysfunctional family. I saw the pain of the family and I knew there were problems, but I always thought, "I know things are tough now, but I want a reason to end happy." You see, it does not matter what you have gone through, (and you are going to go through many tough things in life), you have to learn from it, and grow, and not get bitter. You need to realize that everything you have done, you have created- if not in this life, perhaps in another life.

Learn from people. There is a saying- "People can either be examples or warnings." I think that some people are both. Some people have inspired me, and then when I have taken a little closer look, I think, "Oh my God, I don't want to follow them

Dr. Tedd Koren

in that area." You need to follow carefully, and not follow anything more than what feels right to you. You have to look within, because we can be fooled in our lives. I have been fooled and hurt by people, but you have to keep going and learn from it.

I take care of the Amish. They have a cool Pennsylvania Dutch saying, "You're never too old to learn a new way of being stupid." That is my motto. Always know that you will screw up.

That brings up the issue of failures. Are there any failures in life or are they just lessons to be learned?

The only time you fail is when you give up. I have made so many mistakes, and I have learned from them. Probably some of them I have not learned from, and I am probably going to make more.

> "We sometimes forget that very important lesson, that we became healers to heal ourselves."

Are there any particular failures that you could share with us? What lessons did you learned from them?

No, nothing comes to mind. I try to do what I feel is right. I do not want to sell out to anyone for any reason. I try to develop, as much as I can, a B.S. detector that keeps me honest. That is my goal.

In the publisher's preface of *Think and Grow Rich* it says, "A peculiar thing about this secret of riches is that those who once acquire it and use it, find themselves literally swept on to success, but with little effort. And they never again submit to failure." We would like to hear your thoughts on that.

That sounds good. I like that. You know there are many people that make a lot of money and then die poor. I'm told that most people who win the lottery become bankrupt. I think there would be a wonderful book in that. You know, interview the people and find out how they screwed up. Find out in each chapter how families won millions and then lost it. It depends. Some people go from success to success and some people do not.

Inspire Chiropractic

When I am teaching, I always tell people that the reason I am teaching chiropractors is that I want the doctor to heal himself. Most people become healers to heal themselves, although, most forget this. They forget that they have to work on themselves. Then there are the people who are not aware and are just not conscious of this. Considering the doctors I have seen, I think that is one of the reasons why our profession is such a mess. We sometimes forget that very important lesson, that we became healers to heal ourselves.

Is there a single-most important lesson that life has taught you?

I have learned that chiropractic is no different from other profession. You have some real heroes and some real thieves, and some of them become well known. There are a number of people in this profession that I don't consider honest or sane, and they are in positions of power and influence. Therefore, we have to be careful before we follow anyone, and not take anyone at face value. I have been very cautious in working with others. Thank God that I have had good mentors and teachers because when we were fighting the Federal government and then the Quack Busters. You would be amazed at the people who turned their backs on us. We asked for their help, and they were more concerned that I was not going to name a school or a classroom after them.

Another important lesson is to stay open. I discovered my adjusting technique by accident. The whole idea is to stay open to accidents.

Napoleon Hill talks about the importance of having a Master Mind group. Of people both living and dead, who would you like to have in your Master Mind group?

> "I have attracted many wonderful people that I have a deeply respect. Without them, I do not know where I would be today."

Andrew Carnegie talked about the Brain Trust. You know people

Dr. Tedd Koren

are influenced by the work of others. For example if you read DD Palmer's stuff, you find a lot of homeopathic and osteopathic theory. I do not know if it was conscious or not, but he was strongly influenced by the time and the culture.

I have attracted many wonderful people that I have a deeply respect. Without them, I do not know where I would be today. I certainly would not be where I am now. My wife is one of them. She and my children supported me more than anyone did. I do not think I would have developed the Koren Specific Technique if it were not for my wife. Mainly because she hired the housekeeper that stuffed that big piece of furniture in an odd corner that came crashing down on my head and caused a concussion and ten years of severe pain. That was a blessing in disguise and I am incredibly grateful. Of course, not every experience I have had with my wife has been that painful! She has stood by me at times that required a lot of courage. When we were fighting the Federal government, she was right there. She never hesitated once. The children were great too. I am truly blessed with wonderful children, and I learn from them all the time.

There are people in our profession that have been mentors in terms of teaching their knowledge, philosophy and research. I think I have a habit or a talent for finding incredibly brilliant people in different fields who are often ignored. They do not get the following or recognition that they should have. Jim Turner is one of my best friends. He is the attorney that beat the Federal government fighting the Federal Trade Commission. He also got Life University's accreditation back. Lately, he has been in charge of fighting and beating the Quack Busters. He beat Stephen Barrett and the Quack Busters four times in the last two years. I am the only chiropractor that has ever beaten them. The funny thing is that I find it incredibly satisfying, but if I look to the profession for recognition, I would not get it. It is so political. So I keep going, doing what I think is right, being good to people, and avoiding people that I think are not ethical to deal with. I think that is what we all should do.

I didn't answer your question did I? My most valuable brain trust is composed of my wife, my kids, and my associates. I would also include the doctors that I have attracted to KST and through lecturing on vaccination and philosophy. I am now attracting more than chiropractors- we also have osteopaths and dentists. I have learned from medical intuitive in developing KST- brilliant

Inspire Chiropractic

scientists that are also medically intuitive have come and shown me the path. My lesson from this was to keep your eyes open. Never turn away from anybody, because you never know where the next little bit of insight or wisdom will come from.

Actually, we do not know where we get our insights, ideas and inspirations. Some of the most powerful and important decisions we make in our life, we have no idea deep down why people we decide to love and marry, people we decide to associate with, the types of careers we go into. A lot of it is just inspiration, so we should not turn away from our inspiration. A Mastermind group to me is a source of inspiration. I am not as well organized as some people who actually get together a group of people on a regular basis. I am lucky that we fortunately get to have dinner with the kids every night. That alone is hard enough.

> "Their secrets are not something that they made up. It is something that they have worked at, and when they reach a certain level, they learn from that. Napoleon Hill had no preconceived ideas. He went to people and said, "Show me what works. Show me what makes you successful."

Napoleon Hill lists 13 steps to riches. You have already touched on a few of these, but of those 13 steps is there one that is a favorite of yours?

I think that Napoleon Hill first looked at what works and then he derived his writings from his observations. He went to successful people first. This is very important because this is the basis of what you call empirical philosophy, which is what chiropractic and homeopathic and many other holistic healthcare systems are based on. It is not a matter of intellectually or philosophically deciding what you have to do. It is a matter of doing it and then figuring out what works. So for example, DD Palmer discovered chiropractic because he realized that he did something to someone's spine and his or her health changed and improved. He had many theories of subluxation, and drew things from that, but the first thing was direct experience- the experience of successful healing. Westin Price, a dentist, was probably the greatest nutritionist that ever lived. He went to 14

Dr. Tedd Koren

different isolated cultures in the 1920's to 30's that were perfectly healthy: no cancer, no heart disease, no arthritis, no autoimmune disease, and no mental illness. He went to these cultures and wanted to know why these people were so incredibly healthy. He learned from them. Therefore, I think that the ultimate of Napoleon Hill's work is very spiritual and religious is nature. What he is really saying is, "Perfection in the world is beauty. Success is great accomplishment. There is happiness, fulfillment, and love. Let's go to those people that have discovered this in their lives and find out how they did it." So it is not like an intellectual thing, "Let me tell you my secret of success...blah, blah, blah" It is more like, "This is it. This is how it works. Let's learn our lessons from really good people." I am sure there is a 14th step to riches and that is to have tremendous humility. Because what Napoleon Hill did was, he humbly went before people and said, "Teach me what works." Moreover, I think that this is the essence of what spirituality is- that the world is incredibly loving and spiritual. People have had insights when they saw that the nature of reality is the greatest teacher. Then these same people say, "Let me tell what is. Let me tell you what reality is." Therefore, you have someone who is incredibly happy and successful and you want to know what he or she did. Their secrets are not something that they made up. It is something that they have worked at, and when they reach a certain level, they learn from that. Napoleon Hill had no preconceived ideas. He went to people and said, "Show me what works. Show me what makes you successful." Dale Carnegie did the same thing. He looked at people that were successful and happy and fulfilled. Unfortunately, I do not think he was one of them. We are back to that concept that people become healers to heal themselves, which is not a bad thing. It has been immortalized in literature in many cultures. It is called the "journey of the wounded healer." We are all wounded healers. By learning to heal others, we learn to heal ourselves. Jacob Lieberman, an optometrist, has written some marvelous books on vision; he says that we are each other's homeopathic remedy. Isn't that great? You know people, they give you shit, they give you blessings, they curse you; and as much as they reach you they stir up things inside of you- they awaken things inside of you that you can use for growth and healing.

That is a good motto: We are each other's homeopathic remedies.

Napoleon Hill starts to talk about what will get in the way of

Inspire Chiropractic

you being able to put these steps into practice and he talks about clearing out indecision, doubt and fear. Can you share with us some of the tools you use to clear these enemies out or your way?

I would say he really hit the nail on the head with indecision and fear. You cannot get rid of fear; you just have to do it. I was scared with just about everything I have done. It is like when you learn how to lecture. You are scared when you do it, it can be terrifying even. You might be scared the first time. It is just a matter of doing it. I am still terrified every time. Whenever I fought the government, every time I got a letter, my stomach just tightened up in knots. We beat Stephen Barrett four times in court, but every time I got another serving of papers, I went nuts. I did not go crazy, but I felt horribly uptight. You just do it and it gets better.

I am sure that there are many people who handle things better. Sometimes that is the best reason to have mentors. You know they look at you and say, "Are you an idiot? Why are you doing?" Then you think, "Oh yeah, I hadn't thought of that." One of the tragedies in Chiropractic, I think, is that it did not look like BJ Palmer had many mentors. I think he was terribly lonely. He did not have someone in his life to say, "BJ are you some sort of a jerk or something? Stop doing this stuff." Now I do not want to take away from him, because he did overcome tremendous adversity. He had a horrible father, who was a violent person. He had no mother who loved him. As he grew up he pushed everyone away from him, and yet he still kept a deep faith. I am not trying to come down on BJ, but the truth is you need people in your life who will look at you honestly, and help you realize you are making a terrible mistake. Someone to say, "Have you really thought this out?" That is why marriage is so valuable, and kids. In fact, that is probably why God created teenagers!

You may reach Dr. Tedd Koren at:
www.teddkorenseminars.com

Dr. Tedd Koren

NOTES:

Epilogue

Dr. Bobby Doscher
President and CEO of Oklahaven Children's Chiropractic Center

"A perfect example of the Think & Grow Rich principles is exhibited when the mother has a firm grip on the vision of seeing her child well."
-Dr. Bobby Doscher

Dr. Bobby Doscher is President and CEO of Oklahaven Children's Chiropractic Center, which provides chiropractic to severely sick and handicapped children. Originally founded in 1962 by a volunteer group of six D.C.s as the "Children's Chiropractic Center of Oklahoma," the Center was quickly dubbed "Oklahaven" since it did, indeed, serve as a haven for children and their families, many of whom had been dismissed by the medical profession as beyond help. Doscher -- a Palmer graduate from Philadelphia -- joined the group in 1977 and, under her leadership, the Center expanded to serve even more children, conduct research and to educate people about the benefits of a natural, drug-free health care and the chiropractic way of life. Doscher and her staff have also traveled to Jordan, Guatemala, Poland and Mexico to teach about chiropractic and/or provide services to children in those areas.

Dr. Bobby Doscher

Notes from the editors:

We have chosen Dr. Bobby Doscher to write the epilogue for this book. The association of Napoleon Hill and chiropractic began with the introduction of the world's first chiropractic center for children. Therefore, I feel it is important to end this book with an epilogue from the president and CEO of the Oklahaven Children's Chiropractic Center, Dr. Bobby Doscher.

When we began the development of this book, we also contacted the recently deceased Dr. William Harris. He was Napoleon Hill's chiropractor and friend. Together, they helped promote chiropractic in the early 1960s. W. Clement Stone also was involved with Napoleon Hill and asked Dr. Hill to help build the first chiropractic hospital, which would be named the Kentuckiana Children's Chiropractic Center. Dr. Harris was extremely enthusiastic with our idea for this book, and he intended to do an interview with us. Sadly, just days later, he passed away.

With the publication of this book, I am certain Dr. Harris and Dr. Hill would have wanted to continue leaving a legacy for the chiropractic profession. This small volume is a testament to the success philosophy of Napoleon Hill. It is filled with riches of life, and its philosophy permeates the very substance of what we call chiropractic. Dr. Doscher was instrumental in contacting Dr. Harris before he passed away, and we feel certain that Dr. Harris would want her to have the last words in this most important book for the chiropractic profession.

-Dr. Matt Hammett

Epilogue

I first read *Think and Grow Rich* in the 1960's when I was traveling the world as an International Flight Attendant. This book gave me tools - the power of thoughts, vision, and desire that I needed. I found that I could only save $5,000 it seemed – never getting past it. Therefore, I realized I needed to have another account. I opened another account. Seeing my limitations and using my creative mind allowed me to override

Inspire Chiropractic

my pattern. With this money I was able to enroll in Palmer College of Chiropractic, which would ultimately change my life.

I was reintroduced to the book again as a chiropractic student. When I accepted the position in 1977 at Oklahaven Children's Chiropractic Center and the position of President/CEO in 1979, I remembered the wisdom found in this wonderful book. I reread it to help me ground, direct, and discipline myself to lead the Center and show the way back to health for hundreds of severely hurt children. With time I learned to open one account for each of my needs – bills, house, business, vacation, taxes, personal savings, & investments.

As I look back, it is increasingly obvious that Napoleon Hill's economic principles provided the precise formula that I needed to steer the clinic through the years, and I came to realize that they were also the same principles needed for the mother of the severely ill child to regain health and an abundant life.

From the very beginning, Oklahaven has attracted only parents of profoundly hurt children. These mothers came with faith that there was hope for their children to be well. It was my job to encourage the inner vision of each of these special mothers to see her child obtain his health, reach his full potential, and be able to give back to life.

At Oklahaven, we know that each child is an individual gift with an undeveloped potential. It is vitally important that the parents see the spirit of the child inside and be unwilling to accept labels or diagnoses such as failure to thrive, cerebral palsy, or the autistic spectrum but instead see the wholeness of the child. Chiropractors believe that labels are limiting and that the subluxation, or lack of power within the body, is the root cause of dis-ease which shuts down the innate intelligence of the body. We believe in the power of the adjustment which allows the body to heal itself.

Because the chiropractic premise is often foreign to new patients, education is one of our first tasks. Simply understanding that the "the power that makes the body, heals the body" is the first major step. The chiropractic premise refers to this power as the innate intelligence because it is within the human body. I have seen this force restore wholeness to the most profoundly hurt child. The body regains its power and then balances itself, restoring function and then full function.

Dr. Bobby Doscher

A perfect example of the Think & Grow Rich principles is exhibited when the mother has a firm grip on the vision of seeing her child well. At this point, she is ready to embrace the chiropractic lifestyle for her child. We have observed the mothers achieve this goal when they took their power back and did not allow fear to enter, created a plan, found the way to make the time, and money for the frequent adjustments, to buy and prepare the whole foods and to take care of her entire family.

This special mother knew in her heart that she could not be rich in spirit, life, or money while her child was dysfunctional. She realized that her main duty was to give service and to heal her child. No one else could - not the medical community or government aid, but only the mother's desire and unwavering faith in her child.

She had to be persistent and self-reliant guarding against allowing fear, discouragement, other's thoughts or comments, or a seemingly easier journey to take her off her path. Her greatest ally was her inner vision of her child reaching his optimal potential. She had to learn to stay in the moment to have the discipline to control her mind and dispel the many fears – real or unreal. Her challenge was neither looking back nor fearing the future but giving the joy of service to her child and family.

This is not an easy journey with its ups and downs, which we call "the rollercoaster." This could include the child's behavior, bodily discharges (diarrhea, vomiting, fever, seizure), husbands losing jobs or leaving her and the family. This special mother had to learn how to care for her entire family, yet stay focused on her profoundly hurt child. This is why I call these mothers the "Holy Ones." Their path is tough, but they stay true to the course with inner vision giving them wisdom and freedom.

Yes, many others tried to discourage or persuade her to abandon this journey, especially family and friends, but she remained committed to the path and believed in the greater force of life. Ultimately with her persistence, she was shown the way each time she faced these challenges.

Her determination and strong sense of gratitude gave her an appreciation for the small changes, which led to the big changes. Through this she discovered the natural growth process of her child, the responsibility of parenting, the love of God, and the gift

Inspire Chiropractic

of life. All of this brought about a more abundant life.

Oklahaven Children's Chiropractic Center will celebrate its 50th anniversary in 2011. All of our work has been accomplished privately without state, federal, or United Way funding. The tenets of Napoleon Hill's book "Think & Grow Rich", have allowed children and their families to grow into a more abundant life. As in his book, their journey to health began with a thought, a desire, and a vision to accomplish the seemingly impossible.

I have been honored to see the vision in the mother's eyes, the miracle each day of a child hearing, seeing, walking, or talking for the first time, and the vision of individuals who believed in the children. I am grateful to Napoleon Hill for giving me the formula not only to improve my life personally, but to share his insights and wisdom with the world, especially for the profoundly hurt children.

You may reach Dr. Bobby Doscher at:
www.chiropractic4kids.com

Dr. Bobby Doscher

The Number 1 Inspirational Chiropractic Books Best Seller
INTRODUCTION BY JAMES BLAIR HILL, DO

INSPIRE CHIROPRACTIC

Based on the Original 1937 Version of Napoleon Hill's Best Selling Classic Think And Grow Rich

Includes Special Interview with Mark Victor Hansen
Co-Creator of The Chicken Soup Series

Dr. Matt Hammett
&
Dr. Trish Hammett

www.InspireChiropractic.net

www.ingramcontent.com/pod-product-compliance
Lightning Source LLC
Chambersburg PA
CBHW032259150426
43195CB00008BA/512